IMAGES
of America

SAN DIEGO'S
NORTH ISLAND
1911–1941

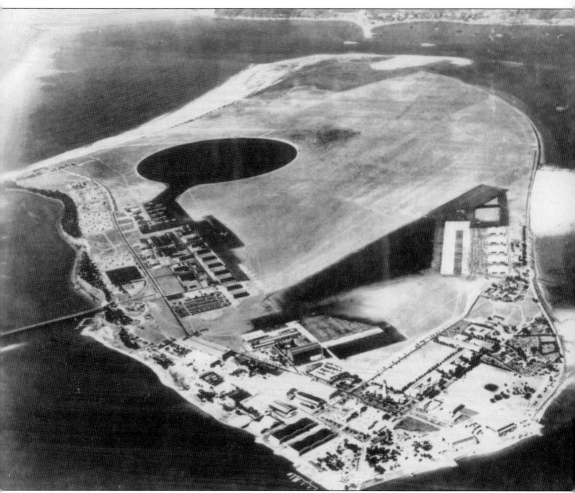

Pictured in this aerial view is North Island in the early 1930s. Visible in the upper left corner is the circular landing pad at Rockwell Field. The Naval Air Station is located in the lower right.

ON THE COVER: This aerial view of North Island looking southwest was taken *c.* 1932. Tied up at the navy's pier are the USS *Langley* and a Bird-class small seaplane tender—likely the USS *Avocet*. *Langley* carried 32 planes at this time, and 28 of them appear on deck. At the time, all of the landing fields on the island were still dirt, although some cement hardstands had finally appeared in front of the training and lighter-than-air (LTA) hangars. (Courtesy of the San Diego Air and Space Museum.)

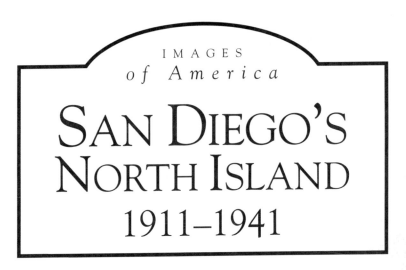

IMAGES
of America

SAN DIEGO'S NORTH ISLAND
1911–1941

Katrina Pescador and Mark Aldrich
San Diego Air and Space Museum

ARCADIA
PUBLISHING

Published by Arcadia Publishing
Charleston SC, Chicago IL, Portsmouth NH, San Francisco CA

Printed in the United States of America

Library of Congress Catalog Card Number: 2007925813

For all general information contact Arcadia Publishing at:
Telephone 843-853-2070
Fax 843-853-0044
E-mail sales@arcadiapublishing.com
For customer service and orders:
Toll-Free 1-888-313-2665

Visit us on the Internet at www.arcadiapublishing.com

*Dedicated to Adm. Joseph Mason "Bull" Reeves,
the true father of modern naval aviation.*

CONTENTS

ACKNOWLEDGMENTS

We would like to thank the staff and volunteers who helped with the research of this publication. Special recognition is given to Alan Renga, who was an invaluable help in editing and scanning images. We would also like to thank our families for their support and patience, making this publication possible. All images used within this book are from the archives of the San Diego Air and Space Museum.

INTRODUCTION

Located in the middle of scenic San Diego Harbor, North Island was once a pair of islands known as North and South Coronado. In 1886, the area was purchased by a developer for a residential resort, and South Coronado became the city of Coronado, while the north portion of the island remained undeveloped. When renowned aviator Glenn Curtiss visited San Diego in 1910, he was immediately attracted to North Island. The island's size, flatness, and year-round ideal climate appeared to Curtiss to be the optimal place for a flying school. A year later, he opened a flying school on the island and held a three-year lease to the property. Soon Curtiss was teaching both military and civilian pilots how to fly. Many of his students would go on to become famous.

In 1914, another famous aviator, Glenn Martin, demonstrated his "pusher" aircraft over the island. This flight included the first parachute jump in the San Diego area, made by a 90-pound civilian woman named Tiny Broadwick. Many other firsts occurred at North Island, including the first seaplane flight in 1911, the first midair refueling on June 27, 1923, and the first nonstop transcontinental flight in 1923.

In 1917, Congress appropriated the land of North Island and commissioned two airfields, Rockwell Field (army) and Naval Air Station (NAS) San Diego (navy). The navy started with a tent-covered city known as "Camp Trouble," but both bases grew quickly, as permanent buildings were soon constructed. By 1918, the army at Rockwell Field had 497 airplanes and over 100 officers. NAS San Diego boasted 76 officers, 110 student officers, and 1,571 enlisted men. The navy shared the island with the army until 1937.

During World War II, North Island was one of the major continental American bases supporting the operating forces in the Pacific. Those forces included over a dozen aircraft carriers, the U.S. Coast Guard, U.S. Army, and U.S. Marines. The city of Coronado became home to most of the aircraft factory workers and dependents of the mammoth base, which was operating around the clock. On August 15, 1963, North Island was granted official recognition as the "Birthplace of Naval Aviation" by resolution of the House Armed Services Committee.

One

FIRST FLIGHTS
1911–1917

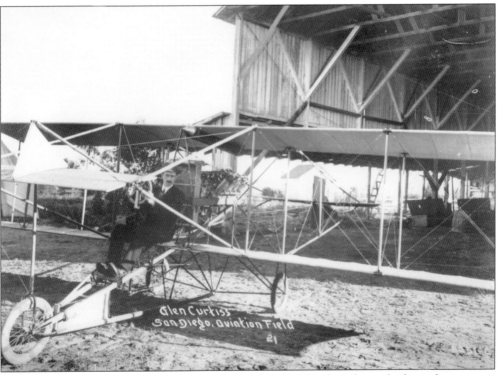

Glen Curtiss
San Diego, aviation Field
21

If there is anyone who would bring notoriety to North Island in the early days of aviation it would be Glenn Curtiss. He would be the first to impact North Island during these years but not the last. Glenn Curtiss first learned of San Diego while participating in the 1910 Air Meet in Los Angeles. Curtiss had been conducting his aviation experiments and flight instruction at Hammondsport, New York, but the winters there made it impossible to fly year-round. Word of North Island's ideal climate and isolated location attracted Curtiss. In early 1911, Harry Harkness, a wealthy New York businessman, formed the Aero Club of San Diego and sponsored an aviation venture with Curtiss. Together they signed a three-year lease agreement, at no cost, with the Coronado Beach Company for the use of North Island. Curtiss is seen sitting in one of his early pusher designs soon after building his first North Island hangar.

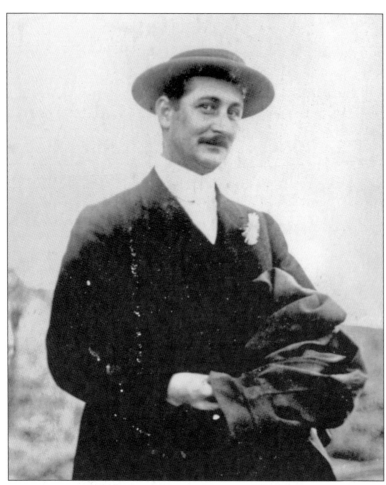

Harry Harkness housed three French-built Antoinette airplanes on North Island. The image below is of two of the unique monoplanes next to Walsh and Curtiss biplanes. The image was taken by Waldo Watermann from the roof of Harkness's hangar.

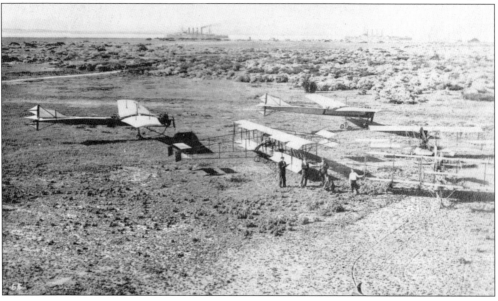

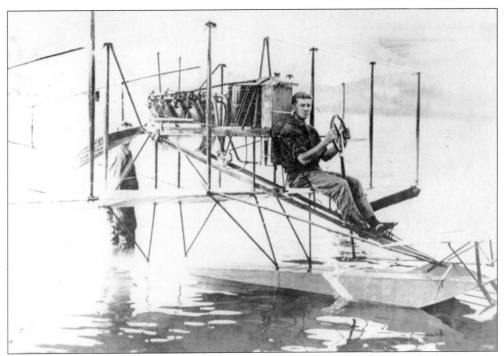

In an attempt to interest the military in aviation, Glenn Curtiss extended an offer to both the navy and army for free flight instruction. The navy was the first to respond, sending submarine officer Lt. T. G. Ellyson to the Curtiss Aviation camp at North Island on January 17, 1911. He became the first naval aviator.

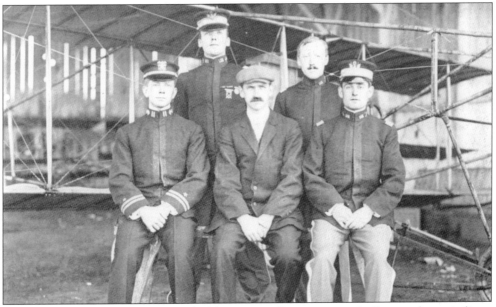

The flight school's first class consisted of three army officers, one naval officer, and two civilians. Seen here are military students at the Curtiss Aviation School in March 1911. From left to right are Theodore Ellyson, navy; Capt. Paul W. Beck, army; Glenn Curtiss; Lt. G. E. Kelly, army; and Lt. John C. Walker, army.

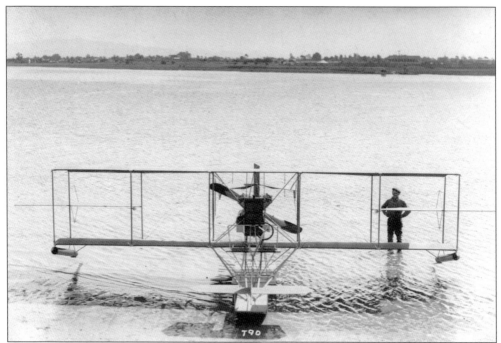

In addition to flight training, Curtiss also conducted numerous aerial experiments. On January 26, 1911, Curtiss accomplished the first successful seaplane flight in the United States. This Curtiss D eight-cylinder landplane was modified with floats in place of its wheels. At one time, the aircraft was modified to a single pontoon instead of three.

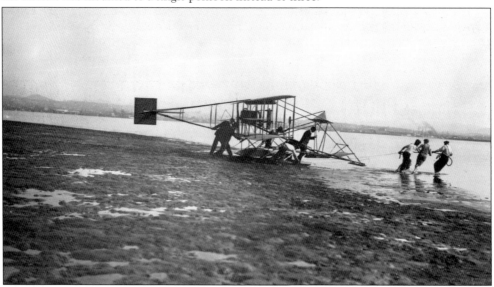

The single-pontoon aircraft was demonstrated to the public at San Diego's second air show on January 28, 1911. One thousand five hundred people filled the grandstands, with thousands more coming to see the show. Curtiss flew from North Island along the coast, crossed Spanish Bight, and landed at the Coronado Country Club polo grounds. The main event was a five-lap race between Curtiss-trained pilots Eugene Ely and Hugh Robinson. The air meet created a great deal of local excitement and attracted many new students to Curtiss's flying school.

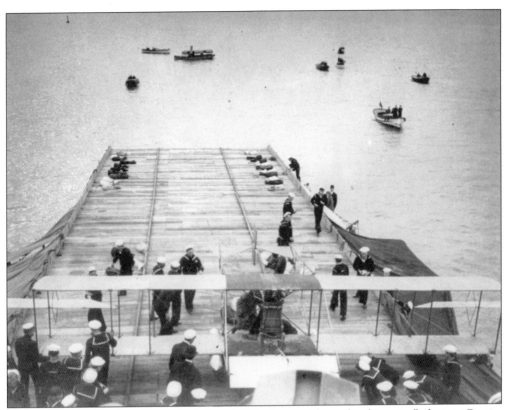

Ten days prior to the San Diego Air Meet of 1911, Eugene Ely made a historic flight in a Curtiss biplane on and off the USS *Pennsylvania* moored in San Francisco bay.

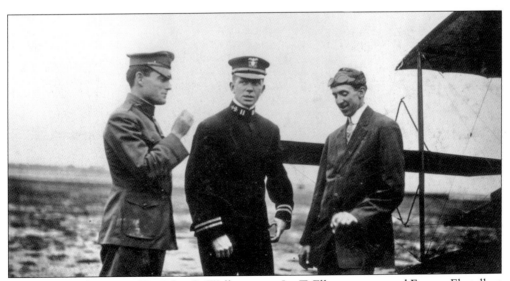

From left to right, Second Lt. John C. Walker, army; Lt. T. Ellyson, navy; and Eugene Ely talk at the Coronado Air Meet on January 30, 1911.

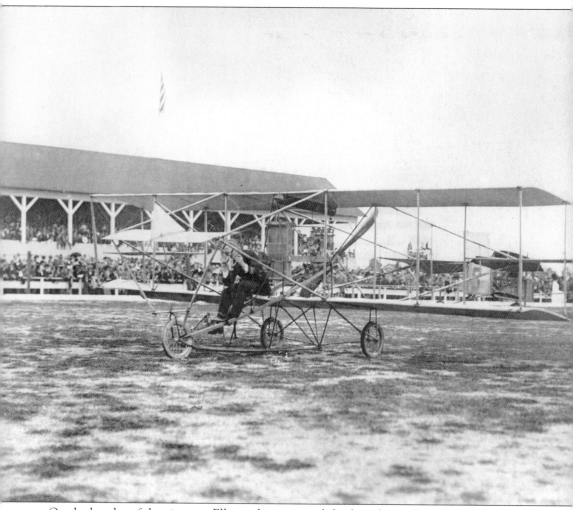

On the last day of the air meet, Ellyson demonstrated the first phase of Curtiss's flight training. The student drives the aircraft up and down the field until able to steer straight and becomes familiar with the controls. The throttle of the aircraft is blocked to prevent enough power for flight. This was only Ellyson's second attempt to drive the aircraft, leading to a minor crack up when he gained 15 feet of altitude and ground looped. Fortunately he was unhurt.

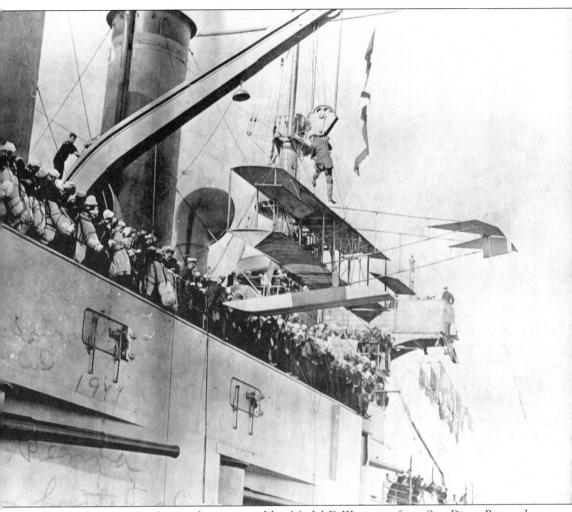

On February 17, 1911, Curtiss demonstrated his Model D-III tractor from San Diego Bay and landed alongside the navy cruiser USS *Pennsylvania*. Curtiss was lifted aboard by a standard boat crane and placed on deck. This demonstration, along with Ely's, was instrumental in showing the navy the feasibility of operating aircraft from ships. Soon afterwards, they announced the first purchase of a navy aircraft.

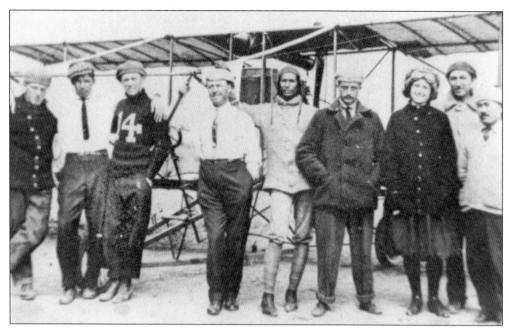

Curtiss attracted a wide variety of students. Pictured here is the Curtiss School of Aviation class of 1912. Included in the photograph are Floyd Barlow, John G. Kaminski, Roy B. Russell, Mohan M. Singh, John Lansing Callan, Julia Clark, M. Dunlap, and Kono Takeshi.

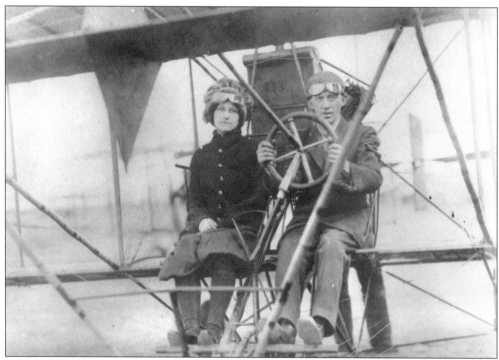

Julia Clark was the first woman student at the Curtiss School of Aviation and the third woman to receive her pilot's license in the United States. She is pictured here with R. H. St. Henry, a fellow student.

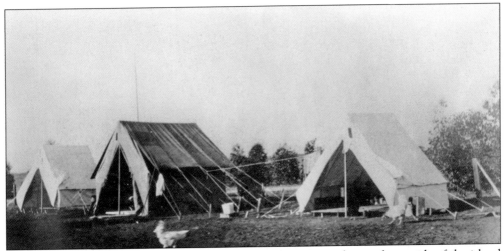

On January 15, 1912, Ellyson set up a temporary navy camp on the northeast side of the island consisting of tents for personnel and three seaplanes. Within four months, all seaplanes had been wrecked, earning the camp the nickname "Camp Trouble." The navy operated alongside the Curtiss school until May 2, 1912, when the detachment was transferred to Annapolis. The navy wouldn't return to North Island until five years later. In the meantime, the army stepped in.

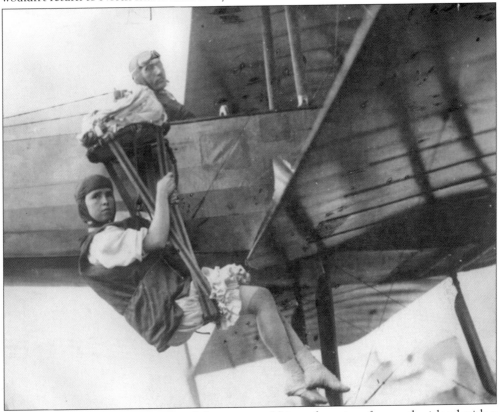

In 1914, Glenn Martin took off and demonstrated his pusher aircraft over the island with a flight that included the first parachute jump in the San Diego area. The jump was made by Tiny Broadwick.

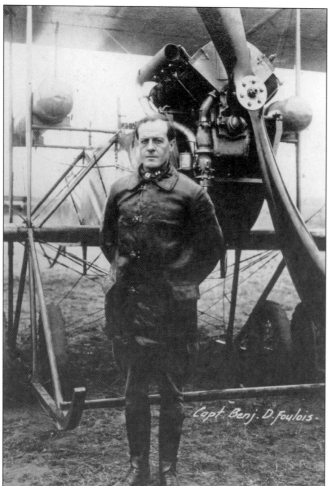

The U.S. Army 1st Aero Squadron was organized at North Island under the direction of Capt. Benjamin D. Foulois, known as the "father of U.S. military aviation." The squadron was the first flying unit from America to reach France in World War I.

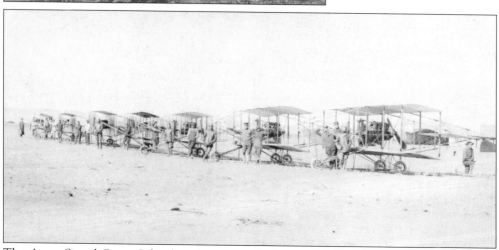

The Army Signal Corps School students proudly line up by their Curtiss Pushers. Curtiss's decision to share the island with the army proved beneficial, because they purchased a number of aircraft from him.

Two

ROCKWELL FIELD
1917–1935

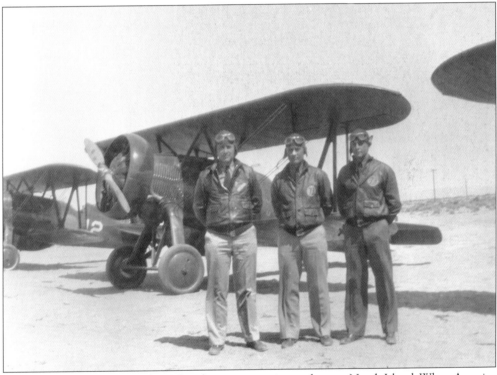

During the years 1917–1935, the U.S. military was growing and so was North Island. When America joined the First World War, Rockwell Field became a center of American army air power on the West Coast. After the war, the field would retain a vital role for the U.S. Army Air Services. During this period, many important aviators and aircraft were stationed at Rockwell Field. Many of these pilots and planes are featured in the following chapter, such as these pilots from the 73rd Pursuit Squadron, 17th Pursuit Group, who are posing in front of their Boeing P-12E fighters at Rockwell Field on North Island. This classic fighter remained in frontline service until replaced by the Air Corps' first monoplane fighters in the mid-1930s. Even then it would continue to serve with reserve units and as a target drone in the early 1940s.

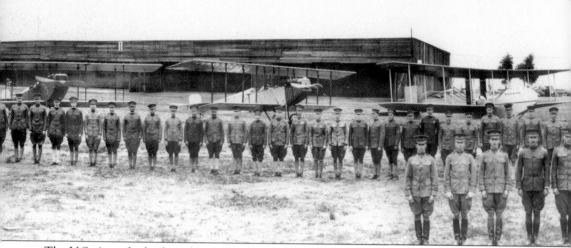

The U.S. Army had a formal presence on North Island almost from the beginning. One of the purposes of Glenn Curtiss's aviation school had been to provide trained pilots for America's armed forces, and officers from both the navy and army were in his first classes. Shortly before the United States declared war on Germany and her allies in 1917, the War Department began looking for a joint army/navy aviation training facility and saw in North Island the same attributes that Curtiss had seen: good year-round weather and lots of flat property reasonably close to a

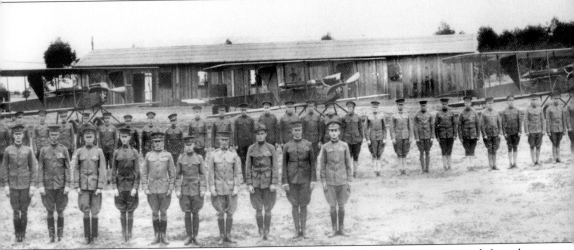

large city with a good transportation infrastructure already in place. The government took formal possession of the island from its owners on August 11, 1917, and proceeded to establish a large training facility with wooden barracks, workshops, storehouses, and hangars. With the end of the war, the military found itself with a reduced need for new flyers but decided to keep the base. The army did not leave until finally relocating to March Field in 1935.

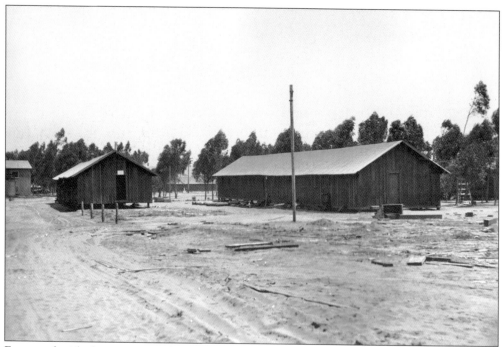

Frustrated with the winter weather at Annapolis, the army began looking for somewhere with better weather for flying. Curtiss extended an offer to the army and they accepted, marking the beginning of the army's 26-year presence. These simple wooden structures were typical of most of the army's buildings on the island.

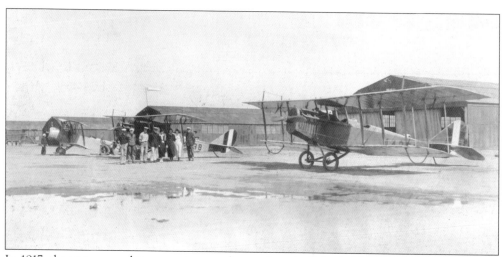

In 1917, the army moved its operations to the south end of North Island to make room for the navy. Seen in front of the wooden hangars are two U.S. Army Air Corps Curtiss JN-4 Jennies and a Sopwith Strutter. The Strutter and several other widely used British and French types from the First World War were brought to the United States after the armistice to supplement the postwar American air services.

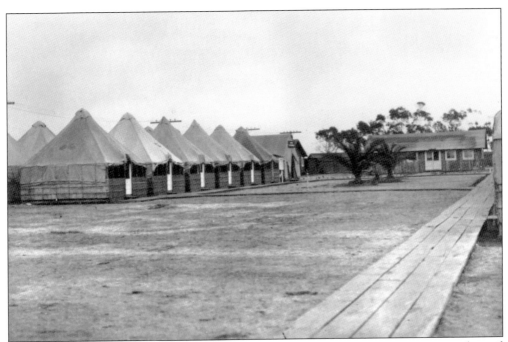

Accommodations for the students and personnel at Rockwell Field were rustic. Most were housed in field tents like those seen in this photograph, while a lucky few were in wooden barracks.

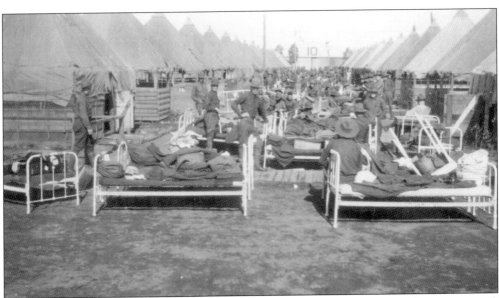

Cleaning the tents meant moving everything out. This photograph shows all of the cots removed, with furniture and gear stacked on top. The soldiers housed in the tents must have appreciated San Diego's climate!

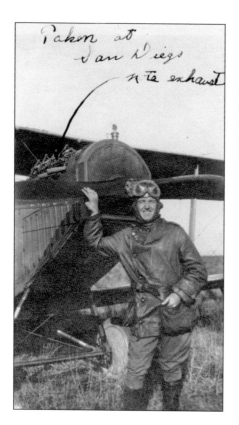

Posing in front of one of Rockwell's Curtiss Jenny trainers is Rueben H. Fleet. Prior to World War I, Fleet volunteered for pilot training with the U.S. Army Signal Corps Aviation Section at Rockwell Field. Fleet's experience as a fledgling aviator in 1917 likely influenced his decision to move Consolidated Aircraft Company in 1935 from Buffalo, New York, to San Diego, California. Consolidated became one of the major aircraft manufacturers in the U.S.

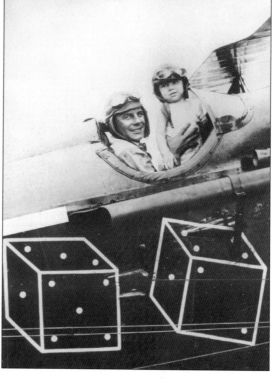

Another famous American with aviation roots on North Island was Jimmy Doolittle. In October 1917, Doolittle enlisted at Rockwell Field. He began setting records on September 4, 1922, when he made the first transcontinental flight from Pablo Beach, Florida, to Rockwell Field, covering 2,163 miles in 21 hours and 19 minutes. Doolittle is seen here with his young son at the start of his cross-country flight.

24

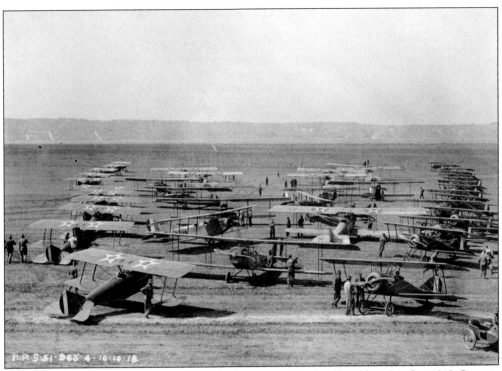

A very busy scene takes place in front of the hangars at Rockwell Field in October 1918. Seen in this photograph are no fewer than 27 Thomas Morse scouts and 15 Curtiss JN Jenny trainers.

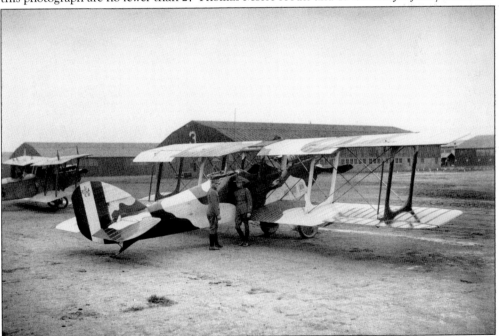

A Packard-Le Pere LUSAC-11 in an experimental camouflage scheme sits in front of the hangars at Rockwell Field. Designed and built during the First World War, only two of the 25 produced were delivered to France before the end of hostilities.

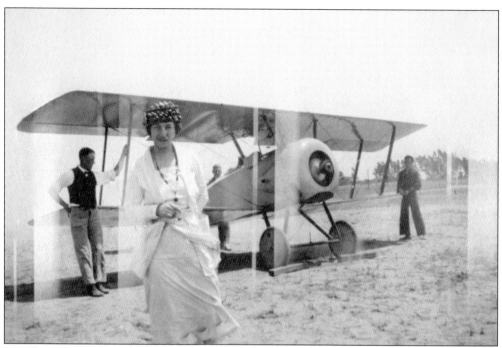

The flying fields of North Island were popular places for the public to visit during the early years of operations there. In this photograph, a young female visitor grins for the camera in front a Thomas Morse scout plane.

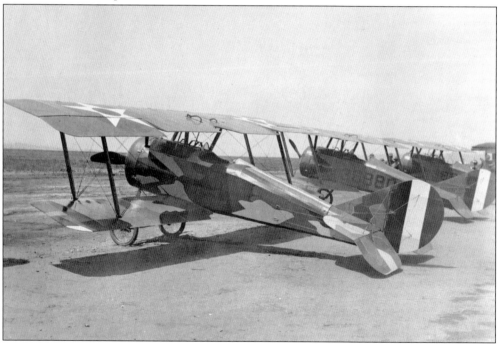

This stunning photograph shows a Thomas Morse scout plane at Rockwell Field in an experimental multicolored camouflage scheme. The wartime roundels have been replaced by the later national markings.

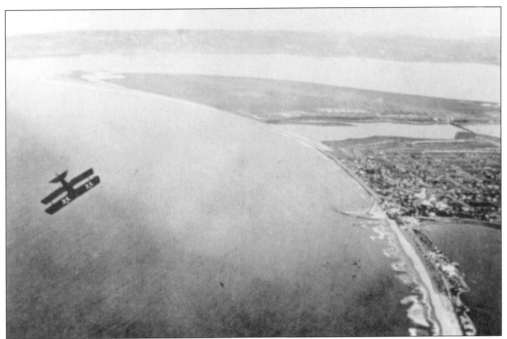

Another photograph shows a Rockwell Field Thomas Morse stunting over the Silver Strand. Coronado, Spanish Bight, and North Island, with Point Loma at the top, can be seen in the distance.

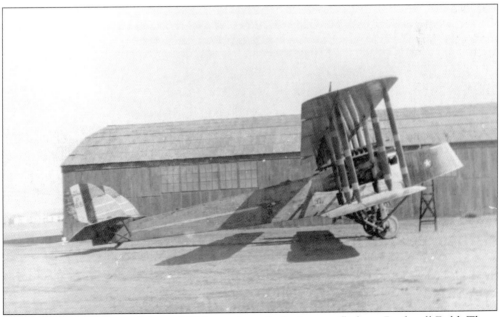

A U.S. Army Air Service Martin MB-1 stands ready for its next flight at Rockwell Field. These Martin bombers were not far removed from the First World War bombers that saw combat, but with the slightly improved MB-2, they served as the mainstay of the army's heavy bomber fleet from their introduction in 1919 until 1927.

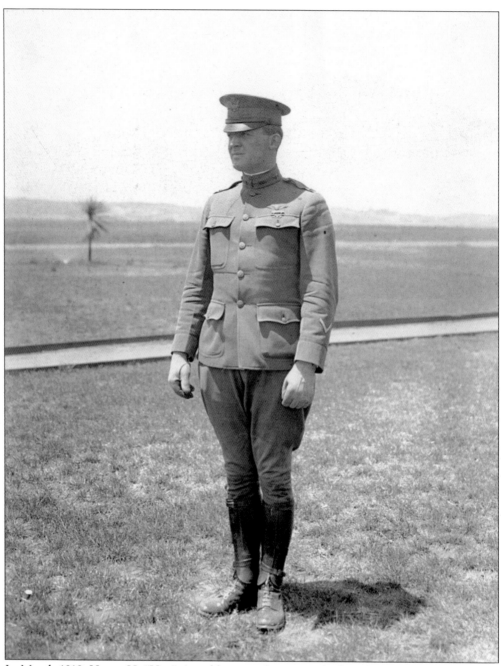

In March 1919, Henry H. "Hap" Arnold assumed command of Rockwell Field. He served at Rockwell Field previously as a lieutenant in 1914 and again in 1916 as a captain. During World War II, Arnold was the commander of all U.S. Army Air Forces. Arnold was a strong proponent of an independent air force.

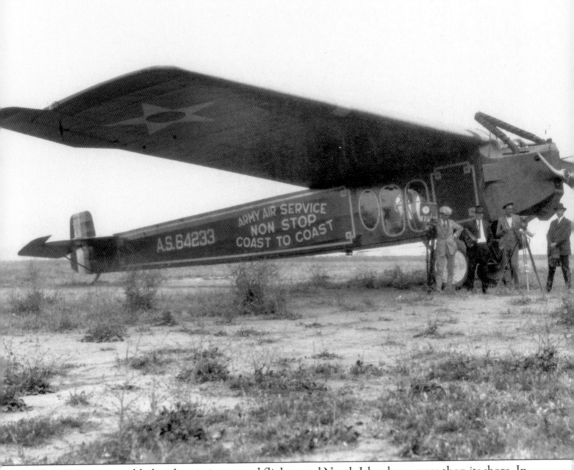

The 1920s were studded with aviation record flights, and North Island saw more than its share. In 1922, Lt. John Macready and Lt. Oakley Kelly, who had been trained at Rockwell Field, attempted to fly nonstop across the United States. This had never been accomplished before. The Fokker T-2 had inscribed along its fuselage, "Army Air Service Non Stop Coast to Coast." The first flight began at Rockwell Field in October 1922 but failed. Ironically they beat the endurance record of 35 hours and 18 minutes. The second attempt ended with a mechanical failure. On their third try, they took off from Hempstead, New York, and ended their flight at Rockwell Field on May 3, 1923, after 26 hours, 50 minutes, and 38 seconds.

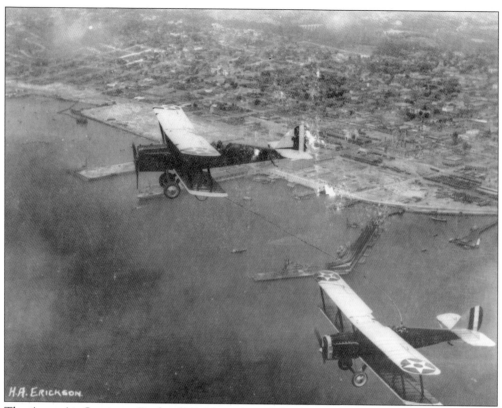

The Army Air Service at Rockwell Field conducted the first midair refueling on June 27, 1923. Capt. Lowell H. Smith and Lt. John P. Richter were in the receiving plane, and Lt. Virgil Hime and Frank Seifert were in the tanker.

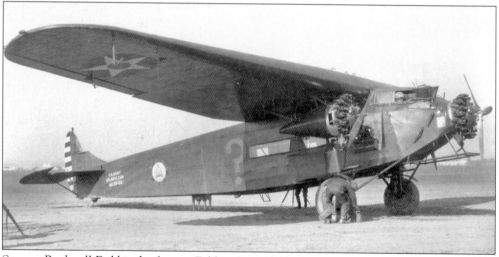

Seen at Rockwell Field is the famous Fokker C-2A dubbed the "Question Mark." This airplane established an endurance record of 150 hours as it circled the San Diego area while being refueled in flight in January 1929. Among its five-man crew were four future generals—Carl A. Spaatz, Ira C. Eaker, Elwood R. Quesada, and Harry A. Halverson—all of whom would play important roles in the development of America's Army Air Force.

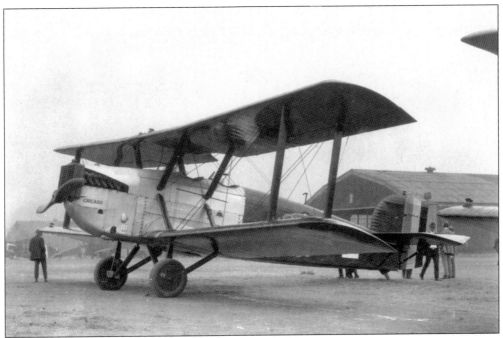

In 1924, the U.S. Army Air Service amazed the world with the first successful circumnavigation of the globe by airplane. Using four specially built aircraft from Douglas Aircraft in Santa Monica, California, the flight was completed between April 6 and September 28, 1924. Two of the original planes were lost during the flight; one, the *Boston*, was replaced by the prototype aircraft quickly dubbed "Boston II." Seen here at Rockwell Field in San Diego is the *Chicago* in September 1924, shortly after the flight was completed. This aircraft was transferred to the Smithsonian Museum for preservation in September 1928.

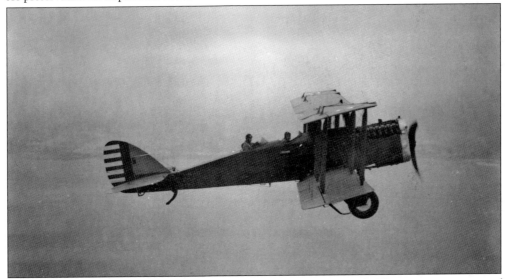

An army DH-4 from Rockwell Field flies over San Diego Bay *c.* 1927. The wartime versions of this British design had a large fuel tank situated between the pilot and observer. This hindered communication and coordinated efforts for the crewmen and exposed them to excessive danger from fire. Postwar versions were redesigned to move the crewmen together.

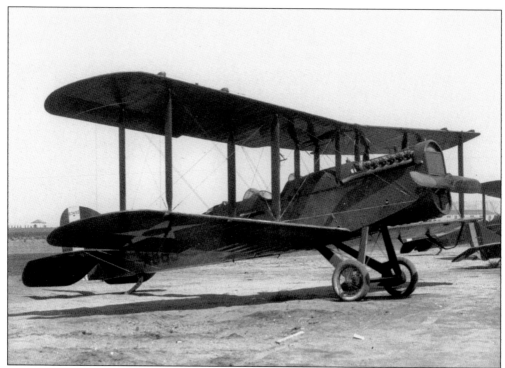

A Boeing-built de Havilland DH-4M-1, serial AS 63485, sits waiting for the next mission on the flight line at North Island's Rockwell Field in 1927. The famous wartime bombers were modernized for the army by several companies, including Boeing and Atlantic (Fokker). All were powered by the American-built Liberty engine.

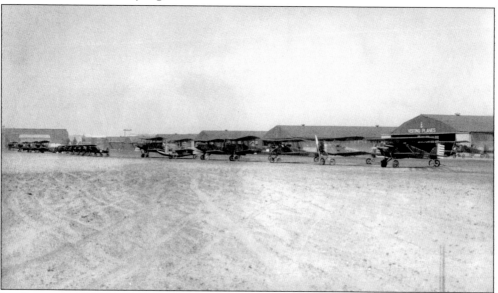

Looking north, this photograph of the army flight line was taken about 1930. At this point, the ramp was still dirt. No fewer than 10 different types can be seen in this view, including a Boeing PW-9, a Consolidated PT-1A and PT-3, a de Havilland DH-4, a Douglas O-2, a Loening OA-1, a Douglas C-1, Boeing P-12s, Curtiss P-1s, and Curtiss B-2s.

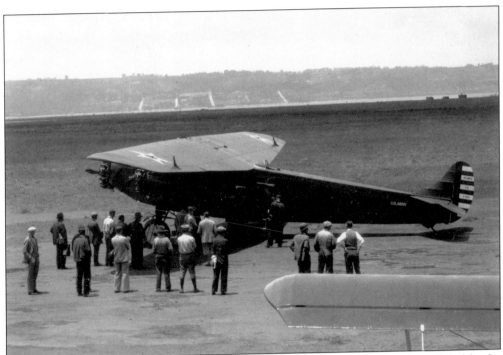

A Fokker-Atlantic C-2, serial P-463, sits on the ramp at Rockwell Field. Specially modified for the flight, the plane, dubbed "Bird of Paradise," flew from Oakland Airport to Hawaii on June 28, 1927. Crewed by Lt. Albert F. Hegenberger and Lt. Lester J. Maitland, this was the first successful flight from the mainland to the islands. Charles Lindbergh called it "the most perfectly organized and carefully planned flight ever attempted."

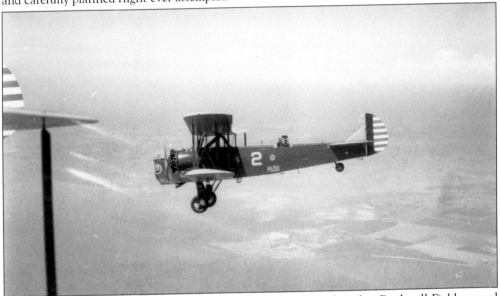

This Keystone B-4A of the 9th Bombardment Squadron was based at Rockwell Field around 1932. Note the movie camera and operator in the rear gunner's position. The B-4A was the last production biplane bomber to be ordered by the U.S. Army. Powered by two Pratt and Whitney R-1860-7 radial engines, the bomber's maximum speed was a stately 130 miles per hour.

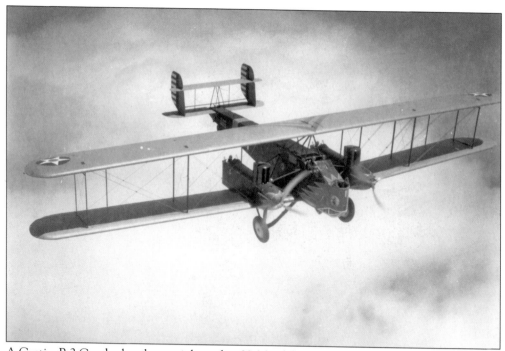

A Curtiss B-2 Condor bomber, serial number 29-36, of the 11th Bomb Squadron is seen in flight over North Island. Only 12 Condors were built, and they were out of service by 1934. The B-2 carried six .30-caliber machine guns and 2,500 pounds of bombs and was powered by two Curtiss V-1570-7 Conqueror V-12 engines, which gave the Condor a top speed of 132 miles per hour at sea level. The rear of each engine nacelle held a gunner's position, and the gunner's heads can just be made out in this photograph.

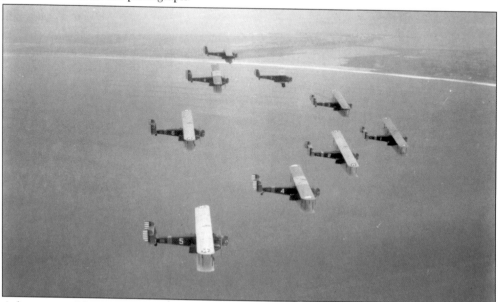

A formation of Curtiss B-2 Condor bombers of the 11th Bomb Squadron flies off the coast of San Diego. Visible in the background are North Island and Coronado. This photograph was taken in 1929, while the squadron was based at Rockwell Field.

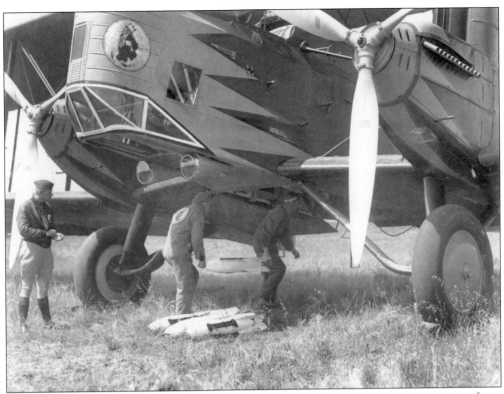

Airmen load practice bombs aboard their B-2 bomber for a training mission from Rockwell Field.

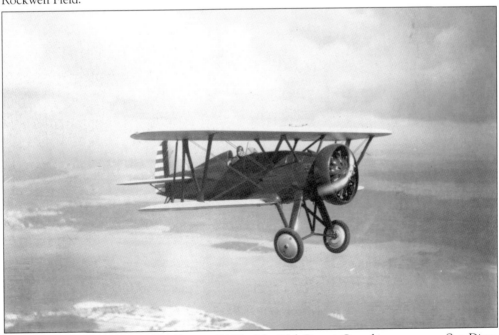

Based at Rockwell Field in 1932, a Boeing P-12E of the 95th Pursuit Squadron soars over San Diego Bay. The army ordered 135 of the model, making it the most widely used of the P-12 series.

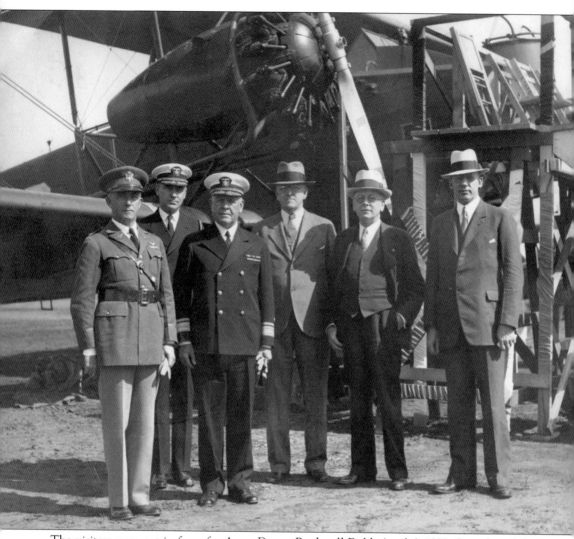

The visitors were out in force for Army Day at Rockwell Field, April 6, 1932. Seen from left to right are Lt Col. Barton K. Yount, Comdr. L. A. Davidson, Adm. Thomas Senn, Allen H. Wright, Mayor Wilson of Coronado, and San Diego mayor Walter W. Austin.

Three

THE FLEET'S IN
1917–1939

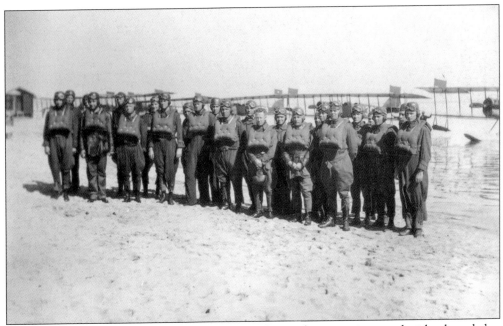

Early in 1918, a decision was made by the army and navy that operations on the island needed to be separated. There were too many differences in operations and techniques to allow for combined training efforts of the two services' aviators. A compromise was reached that allowed the navy to take over the northeast corner of the island while the army relocated to southeast end. All landplane flying operations took place on the western half of the island. Almost immediately, the navy began to plan and build permanent buildings, while the army continued to operate out of temporary wood structures. The following chapter will document the many important people, aircraft, and events that took place on the navy's side of the island. Here Lt. Frank Simpson Jr., the officer in charge of flight school, and a group of pilots and student fliers line up at NAS San Diego on North Island on July 9, 1918. The pilots wear protective helmets, goggles, life vests, and grim faces as they prepare to go flying in the flimsy Curtiss N-9 float trainers seen behind them.

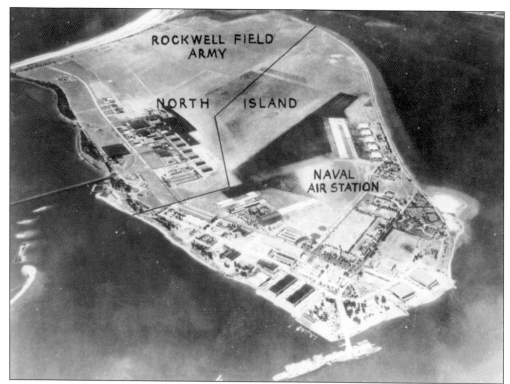

Taken c. 1925, this image of North Island has been marked to show the borders between the army and navy areas of operation. Over the next five years, the flying fields would be further developed.

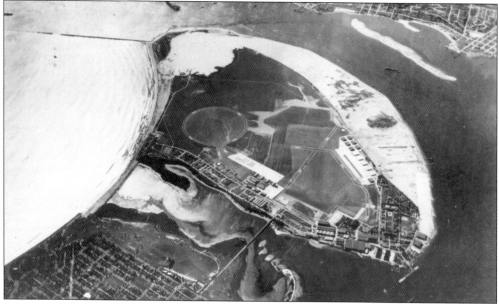

Taken in 1933, this photograph of the island with Spanish Bight in the foreground shows the distinctive round army flying field at the south end of the island, with the navy's rectangular field in the center. The fields were regularly sprayed with oil to reduce dust. Point Loma and the Pacific Ocean are visible at the top of the photograph.

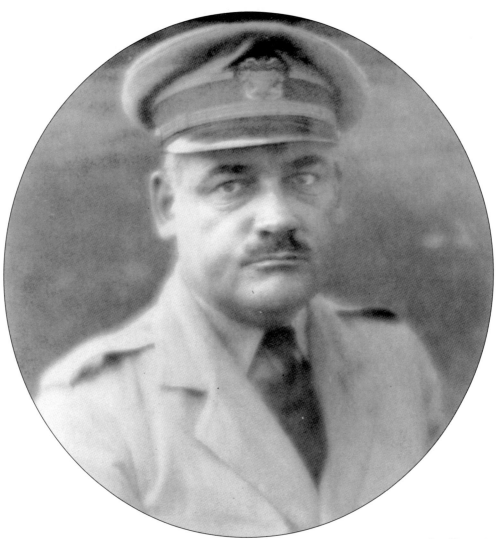

On September 25, 1917, Lt. Earl W. Spencer, U.S. Navy, was ordered to report to San Diego in order to establish a permanent naval air station for training purposes. On November 8, 1917, Lieutenant Spencer became the commanding officer of the naval air station on North Island. Spencer remained in command until December 1919. He married Elizabeth "Bessie" Wallis Warfield in 1916, and they divorced in 1927. Warfield later become known as the woman for whom Edward VIII of England would give up his crown. In 1928, she married Ernest Aldrich Simpson.

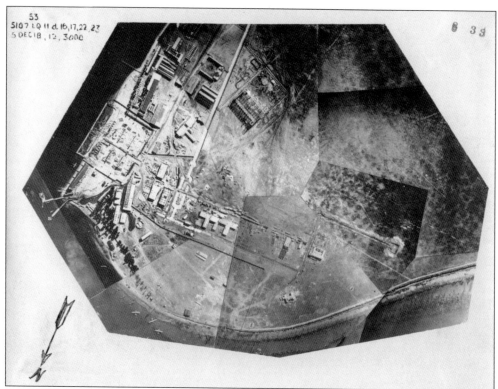

This composite aerial photograph of the north end of the island was taken on December 5, 1918. Construction of the new navy building has begun, with the new lighter-than-air building visible in the center.

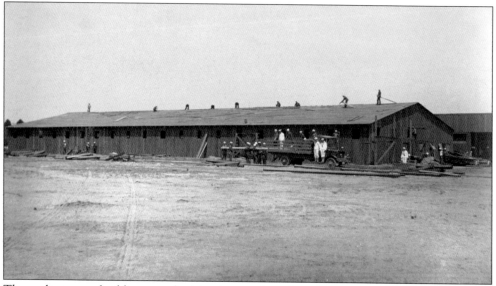

The earliest navy buildings on the island were of similar construction to the simple wooden structures already in use by the army. Made in some cases with wood salvaged from dismantled army buildings, these facilities were intended for use only until permanent buildings were made ready. This June 1918 view shows a new enlisted barracks nearing completion.

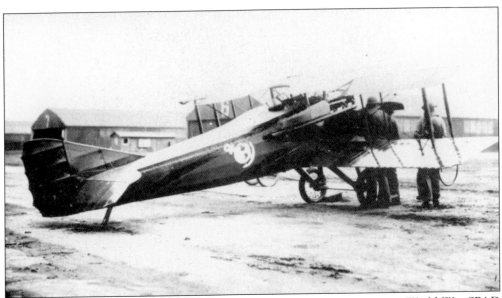

This mediocre-quality photograph is extremely rare in that it shows a First World War SPAD fighter in very early U.S. Marine Corps markings at Rockwell field, c. 1919. One of the most famous French fighters of the war, SPAD XIII fighters were imported to this country after the armistice in large numbers and served as both frontline aircraft and trainers for several years; only a very few served with the marines.

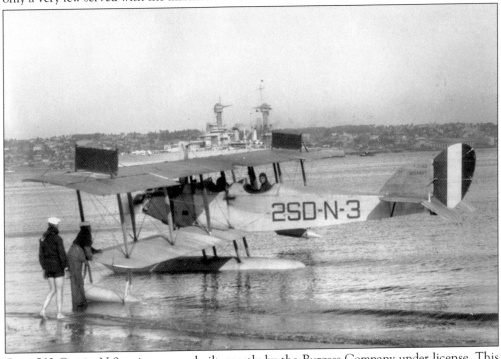

Over 560 Curtiss N-9 trainers were built, mostly by the Burgess Company under license. This World War I type, while very similar to the famous JN Jenny, was designed from the outset as a seaplane trainer for the navy. Seen floating peacefully on San Diego Bay with a battleship at anchor in the background is Burgess-built A-2583, assigned to the base reserve unit.

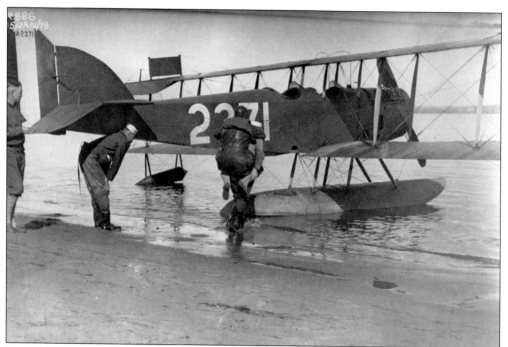

How does an eager young student pilot get into his floatplane trainer without getting his feet wet? Apparently on the back of one of the ground crew! Two of the enlisted personnel in this photograph are wearing deepwater waders as they prepare to launch the Burgess-built N-9H.

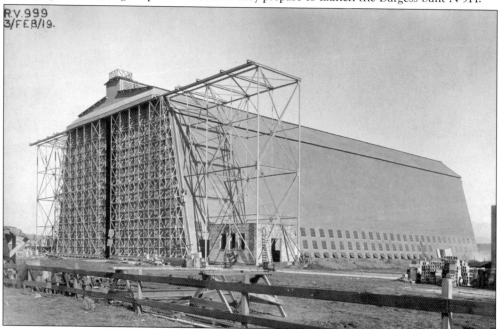

During the last years of the First World War, the navy showed great interest in lighter-than-air technology. North Island was looked upon as an optimal site for dirigible activities. Construction of a dirigible hangar over 250 feet long was ordered. In this February 3, 1919, photograph, the hangar is nearly complete, and the huge doors are under construction.

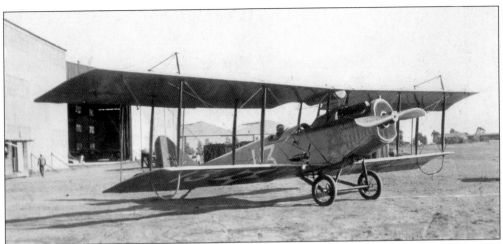

Synonymous with aviation during the years immediately following World War I, the Curtiss JN Jenny served with all branches of the United States military in many forms. This aircraft is a JN-6H and mounts a wind-driven generator on the lower right wing. Note that the underwing stars have been applied backwards.

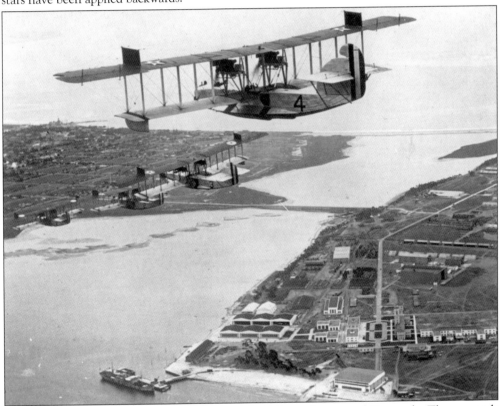

Four F5L flying boats from NAS North Island fly in formation toward Coronado. The numerals atop the wing of the nearest plane have been accidentally applied in reverse. The NAS is in the lower right; the army's Rockwell Field is just visible in the center right. The island was connected to Coronado by the causeway visible in the center. The body of water between them, known as Spanish Bight, was filled in during the 1940s.

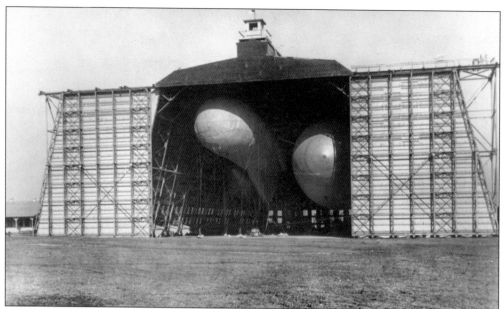

Once complete, this hangar could accommodate all but the largest airships then in service. When the hangar was built in 1919, it was the largest building on North Island. To commemorate the opening, a gala party was thrown whose attendees included numerous Hollywood stars, such as Mary Pickford.

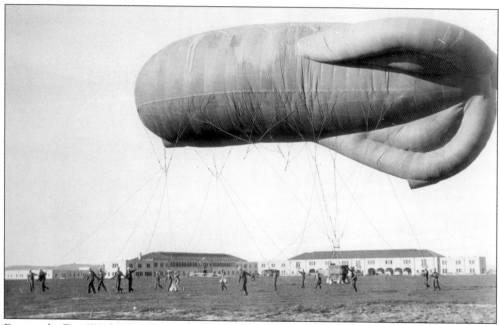

During the First World War, airships played a vital role as spotters and patrol craft. An important part of the training process at NAS San Diego in the early years included lighter-than-air instruction, as the military was convinced that the type could play a role in protecting the coasts. Several types of airship, both powered and free flight, were used. This 1920 photograph shows a World War I–style observation "kite balloon." The new control tower is taking shape in the background.

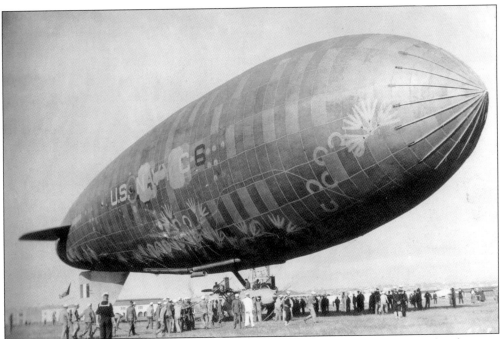

Another type of nonrigid airship used at North Island was the C-series coastal patrol and convoy protection type. Noted for its reliability, 10 were supplied by Goodyear and Goodrich starting in 1918. The C-7, a sister ship to the C-6 seen here at North Island around 1921, was the first airship to be filled with helium instead of hydrogen. Another sister ship, the C-2, became the first airship to fly from coast to coast across America in 1921.

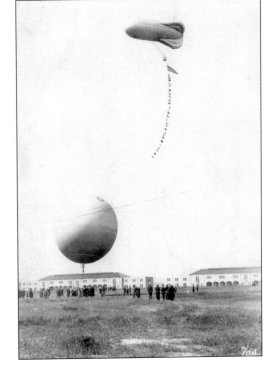

On July 15, 1920, Vice Pres. Thomas R. Marshall visited North Island. In honor of the occasion, a race was staged between three hydrogen-filled balloons. The race was a near disaster, as unpredictable winds sent the balloons in different directions. Each balloon was forced to make an emergency landing, and no winner was announced.

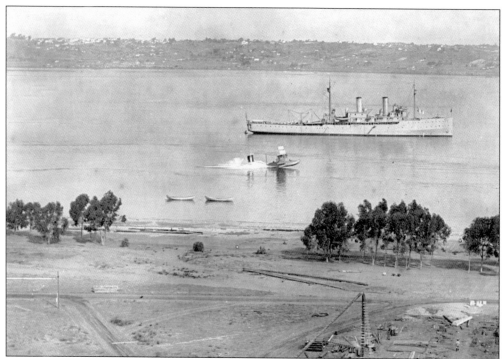

An NC flying boat lands on the calm bay water between NAS North Island and the USS *Aroostook*. The plane was built as the result of a combined effort between the Naval Aircraft Factory and Curtiss, hence the unusual designation. Four NCs became famous for mounting the first aerial crossing of the Atlantic, in stages, in 1919. One of the planes made the flight successfully and is now on display at the Naval Aviation Museum in Pensacola.

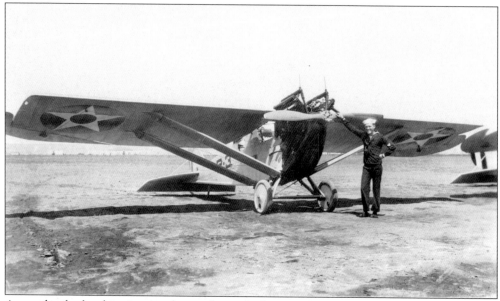

A proud sailor has his picture taken in front of a Loening M-8-1 at NAS North Island *c.* 1922. Designed for the navy just after World War I as a pursuit plane, most of these revolutionary two-seat monoplanes were used as observation ships.

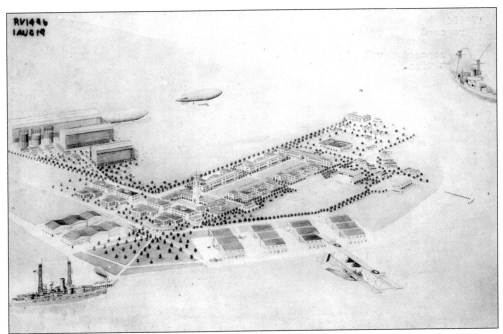

This is an artistic view of the plan for the final configuration of NAS San Diego dating from August 1919. While most of the permanent buildings shown were finished and the configuration would remain unchanged, only one of the three planned lighter-than-air hangars would be built.

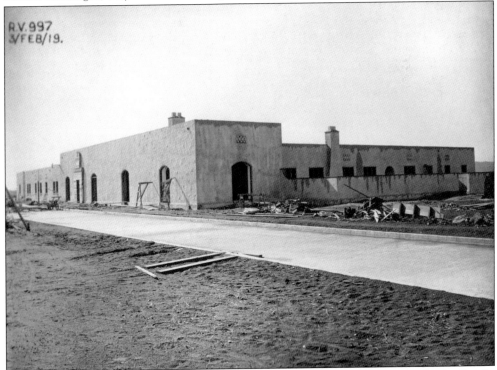

Seen here under construction in 1919, the bachelor officers' quarters on North Island offered a comfortable home away from home.

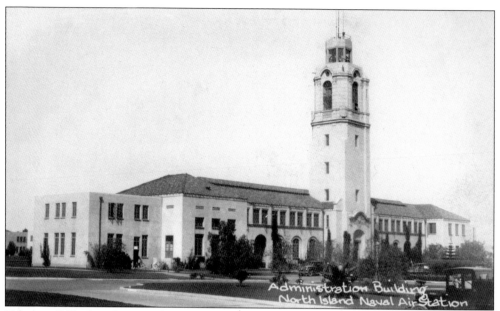

Taken *c.* 1925, this photograph shows the newly completed base administration building with its control tower. Although there is a new control tower today, this distinctive building remains in use.

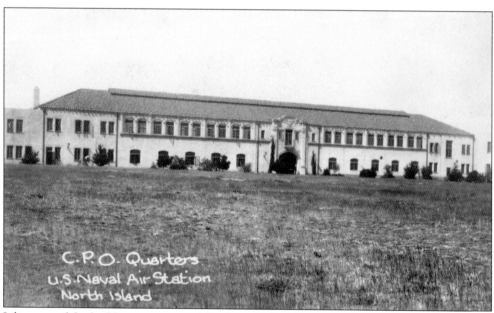

Like most of the buildings constructed for the navy between 1918 and 1930, the old chief petty officer's building is still in use today. This view was taken *c.* 1925.

48

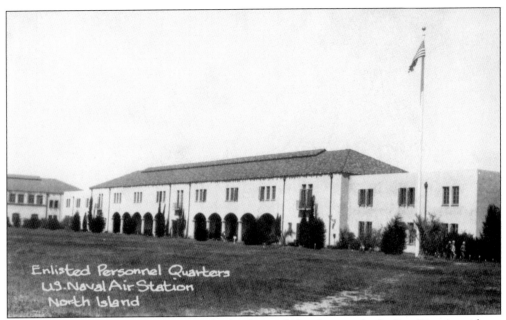

The construction taking place on North Island provided welcome jobs for San Diego's residents and a significant boost to the local economy. Also taken around 1925, this photograph shows one of the barracks for enlisted personnel.

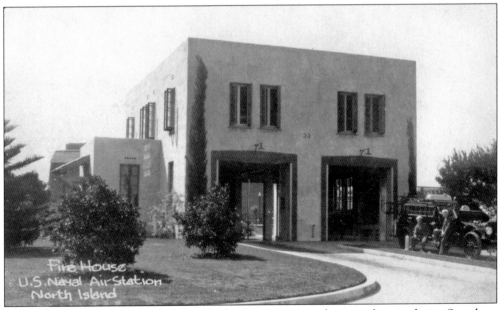

Like a small city, the base needed all of the basic services in order to perform its duties. Seen here in 1925 is the new base firehouse.

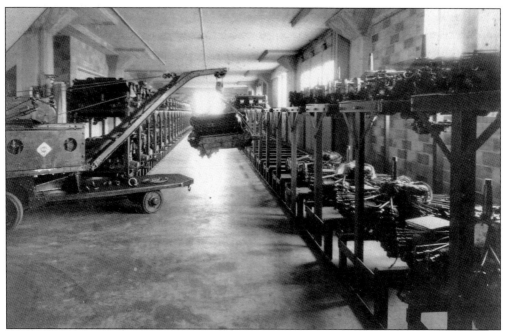

In addition to housing and administrative buildings, North Island boasted the best fleet aircraft repair and maintenance facilities on the West Coast. This photograph shows part of the Curtiss engine shop, with a small portable crane moving a Conqueror engine to its storage rack in the center.

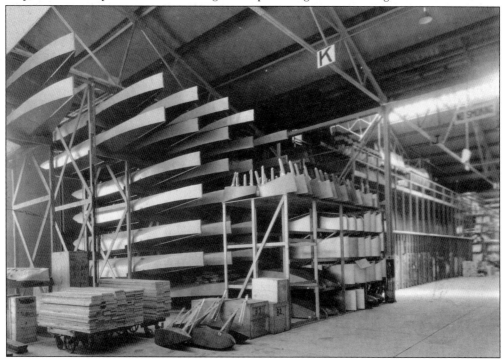

Part of the float storage area in one of the base warehouses is pictured here. Seagoing operations, whether from the water or the decks of carriers, were hard on airframes and engines, so the navy's maintenance personnel had to be ready to replace or rebuild just about every part on a plane.

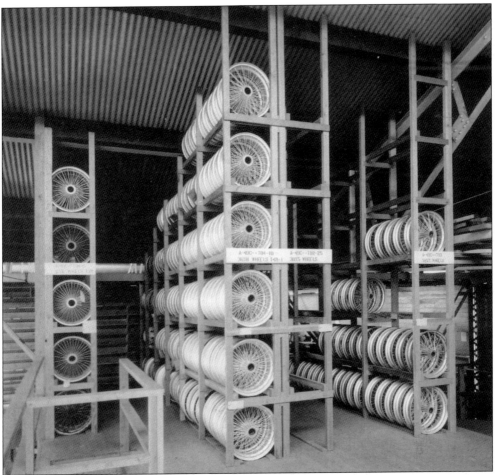

Another warehouse view shows spare wheels for T3M and T4M torpedo bombers.

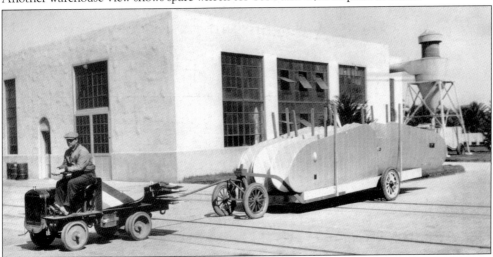

A small gasoline tractor, driven by a civilian base employee, is seen with a load of lower wings and rudder assemblies. If called upon, the base facilities could build entire airframes from parts.

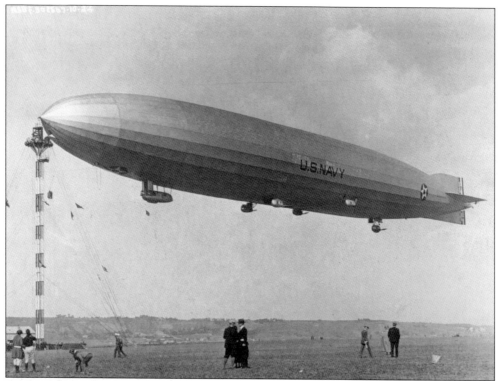

On October 10, 1924, the navy's first rigid airship, the giant USS *Shenandoah*, paid a visit to San Diego and landed on North Island. The army assisted in mooring the dirigible at Rockwell Field.

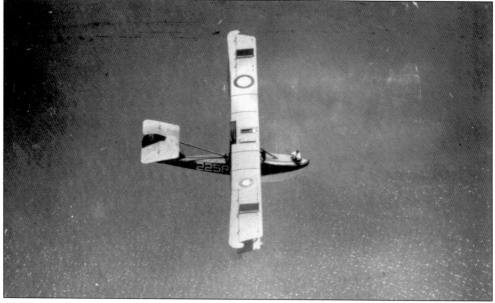

This North Island–based Curtiss HS-2L still carries wartime roundels above the wing in two different sizes *c.* 1925. HS-2Ls were the first American-built planes to be flown by U.S. Navy forces in France during the conflict. They remained the standard patrol and training flying boat in the navy after the war and did not leave service until 1926.

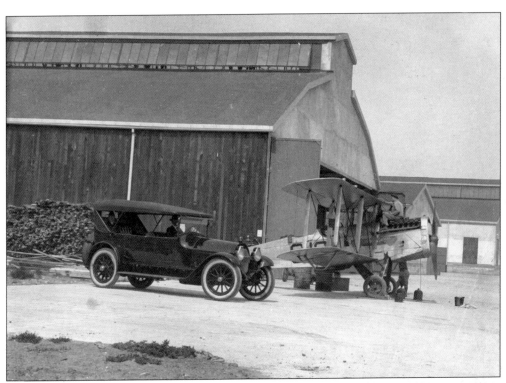

Parked next to one of North Island's early wooden hangars is a de Havilland DH-4B assigned to the base photographic unit. Next to it is a then-new 1919 Locomobile Model 48 touring car. The DH-4 was a rugged, all-purpose aircraft that had been designed in England during the First World War and was built in large numbers under license in the United States. The type managed to soldier on well into the late 1920s.

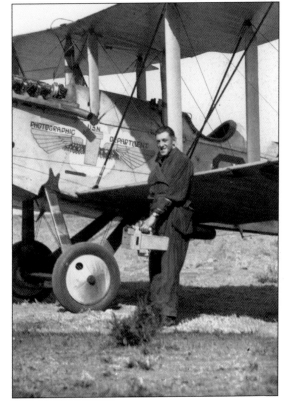

Many of the photographs in this book were taken by Chief Photographer's Mate J. M. F. Haase. Haase was the senior photographer at North Island from roughly 1922 to 1932. During this time, he participated in a remarkable number of significant events and firsts. This photograph shows him leaning against the aircraft assigned to his unit. The San Diego Air and Space Museum archives now holds a significant collection of Haase's original negatives.

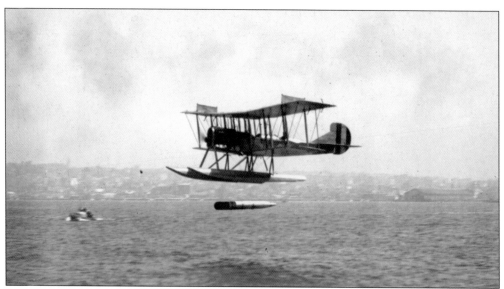
A practice torpedo is dropped in San Diego Harbor by a Curtiss R-6L in 1921. These ungainly planes were converted trainers and served as some of the navy's first torpedo bombers.

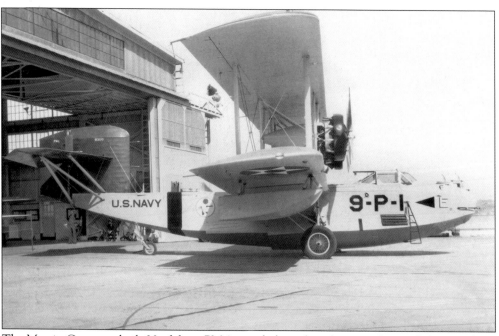
The Martin Company built 30 of these PM-1 patrol planes based on naval aircraft factory plans. This aircraft is the commanding officer's plane assigned to VP-9F in 1936.

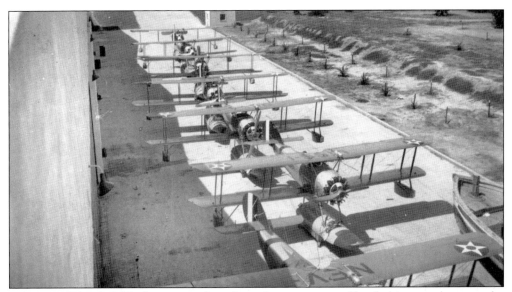

A lineup of Vought UO observation floatplanes from a variety of battleships rests between the maintenance hangars. Whenever the ships of the U.S. fleet were in port at either San Diego or San Pedro, their aircraft were flown to North Island for maintenance, storage, and training. Abbreviations for the ships names appear on the upper wings. Visible in this view are planes from the *Nevada*, *Mississippi*, and *Oklahoma*.

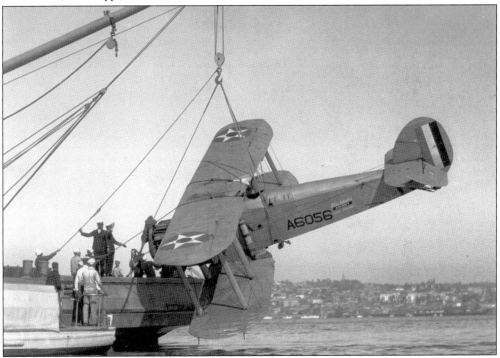

This ungainly looking plane is a Blackburn Swift. Developed by the British as a torpedo bomber, two were purchased by the U.S. Navy for evaluation in 1921. The planes were powered by a Napier Lion engine. During testing, this aircraft suffered engine failure and crash-landed in San Diego Bay.

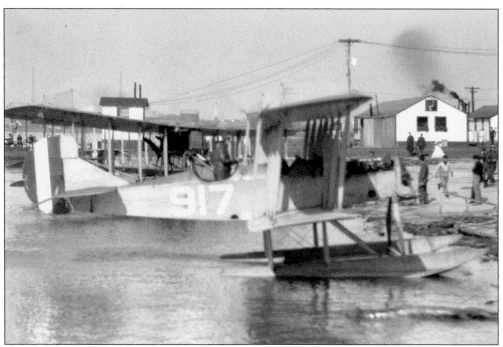

The Curtiss R-6 was built during World War I and was used for observation, scouting, and training by the army, navy, and Royal Air Force. Some were even modified to carry naval torpedoes. This plane is seen in service as a trainer assigned to NAS North Island *c.* 1925.

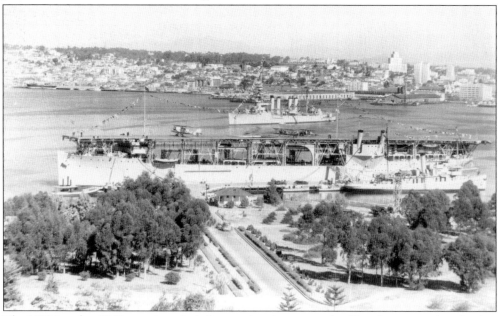

The USS *Langley*, CV-1, was America's first carrier. A converted collier, she was used to develop the navy's fledgling air arm. She is seen here on Navy Day 1929 at her dock at NAS North Island. Among the planes visible on her deck are a UO-1 and a Martin T4M-1 from the torpedo squadron VT-1B. The latter must have been visiting from the USS *Lexington*, as *Langley* did not carry a torpedo squadron at the time.

Adm. Joseph Mason Reeves was instrumental in the development of carrier aviation. At the age of 53, Reeves qualified as a naval aviator observer and became the first officer wearing wings to be promoted to flag rank.

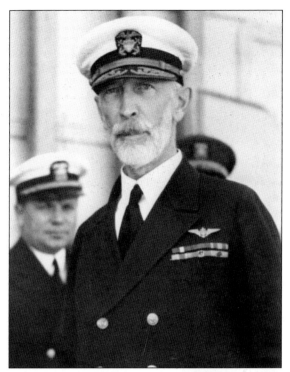

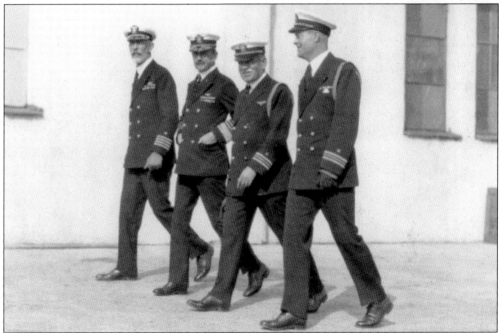

In October 1925 Reeves assumed command of the Aircraft Squadron, Battle Fleet assigned to *Langley*. At the time, the carrier was classified as an experimental ship and was the only aircraft carrier in the navy. Under his command, he introduced concepts of efficiency that transformed carrier tactics and doctrine. Seen here is Reeves walking with members of his staff at North Island.

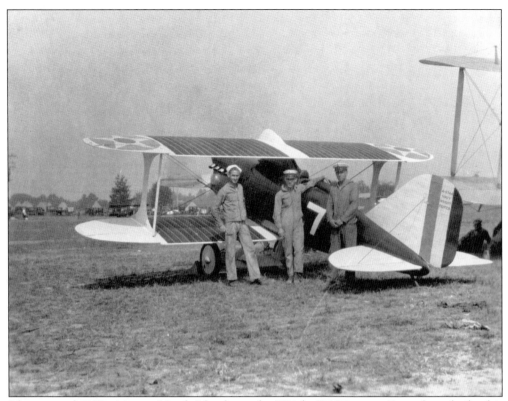

This unusual 1923 visitor to North Island was the Wright F2W-1 racer. One of two built, this airplane was flown to a third-place finish in the 1923 St. Louis Air Race by U.S. Marine Corps lieutenant Lawson H. Sanderson.

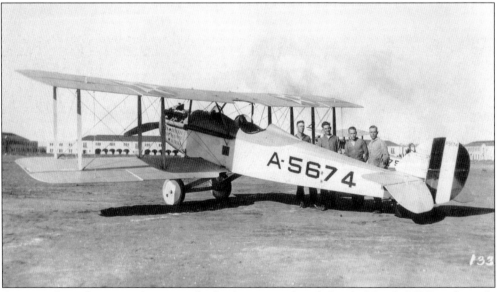

A group of proud navy mechanics smiles for the camera from behind a Vought VE-7 in the early 1920s at NAS San Diego. A capable trainer with the U.S. Army Air Corps and the U.S. Navy, a VE-7 was the first plane to take off from the USS *Langley* on October 17, 1921.

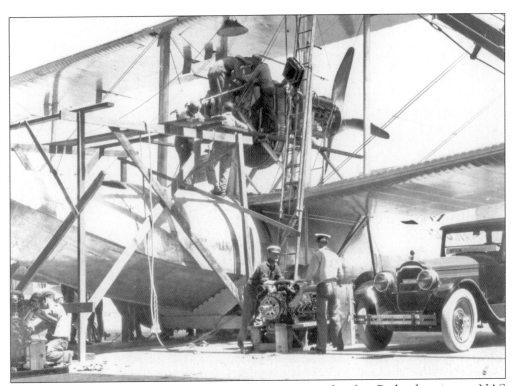

The Boeing PB-1 flying boat receives maintenance on one of its four Packard engines at NAS North Island. A sign on the windshield of the Packard touring car reads "Official Car of the Trans Pacific Flight." In fact, the plane was intended to have accompanied the Naval Aircraft Factory PN-9 on its remarkable flight from San Francisco to Hawaii during August 1925. Mechanical problems kept the PB-1 from making the trip. The primitive maintenance conditions that existed on the island at the time, as well as the immense size of the flying boat, are very obvious in the photograph.

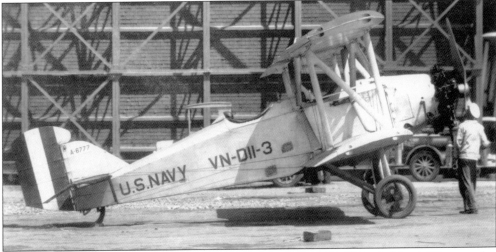

A Boeing NB-2 sits in front of the lighter-than-air hangar at NAS North Island. The complex designator on the fuselage side indicates that the plane is Plane No. 3, assigned to the naval reserve squadron in District 11.

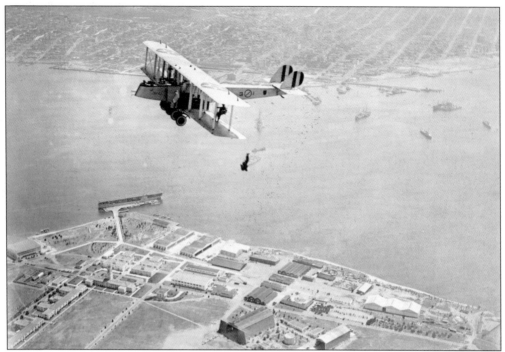

Formed in 1925 at San Diego, the U.S. Marine Corps' 2nd Aviation Group operated an eclectic mixture of aircraft, including at least two Martin MBT heavy bombers. This 1926 image of A-5716 illustrates the primary use the marines seem to have had for the big plane: dropping parachutists. This aerial view gives a good idea of how the naval portion of North Island was laid out at the time. Note also the USS *Langley* tied up at the carrier pier.

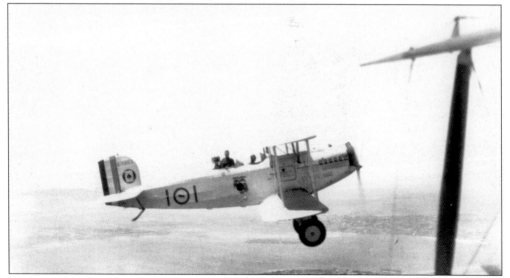

A VO-1M Douglas OD-1 forms up on the camera plane over North Island in 1928. While various versions of this type served in large numbers with the army, only two of these planes were built for the navy. Both served very briefly with marine observation squadrons before being relegated to utility duty. The aircraft was powered by a 400-horsepower Liberty engine. Note the motion-picture camera in the rear cockpit.

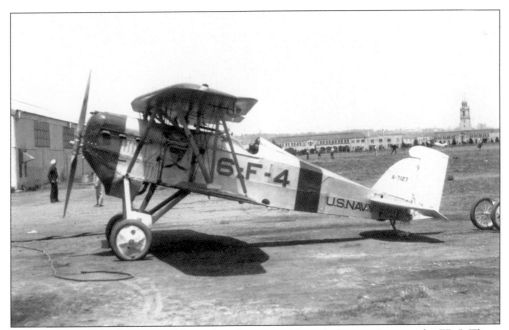

The final Boeing biplane to be delivered to the navy with an in-line engine was the FB-5. These planes were not test flown before delivery. Their first flights were all made during the transit to San Diego from the *Langley* deck. These planes only lasted in fleet service for about a year before being handed over to the U.S. Marine Corps. Seen at NAS San Diego in 1927, this plane is assigned to the VF-6B squadron.

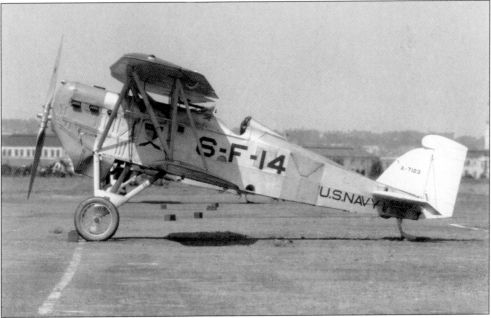

FB-5, Bureau No. A-7123, was assigned to VF-6B off the USS *Langley*. Seen on the ramp at NAS San Diego in 1927, this aircraft has been restored and is currently on display at the San Diego Air and Space Museum. This aircraft appears to have a yellow nose and fuselage band along with the white tail unit.

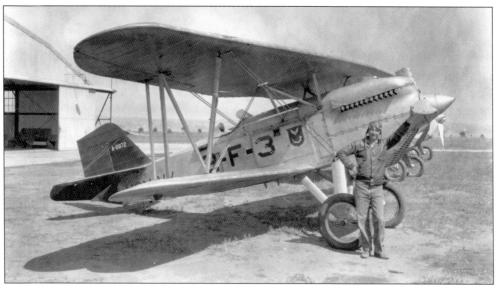

This photograph shows a proud pilot and his Curtiss F6C-1, No. A-6972, assigned to squadron VF-2B as 2-F-3 at NAS North Island in 1926. Along with the Boeing F4B series, the Curtiss Hawk fighters are among the most famous of the navy's interwar planes. The F6C-1 was not equipped for carrier operations but did give the pilots of the day a chance to fly a truly high-performance fighter. Three of these planes were delivered to VF-2B—"Fighting Two"—for evaluation. VF-2B was unique in the fleet in that it was staffed almost entirely by enlisted pilots.

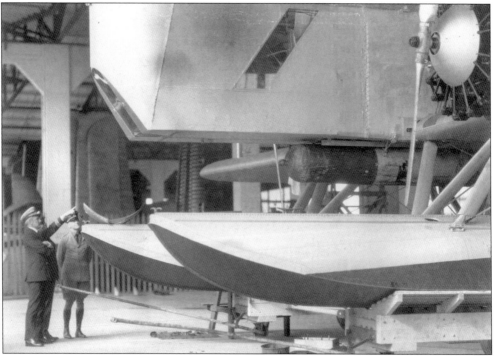

Officers inspect the Douglas XT2D-1 at NAS North Island in 1927. This large twin-engine torpedo bomber could be operated off wheeled gear or floats. Note the dummy torpedo mounted beneath the fuselage.

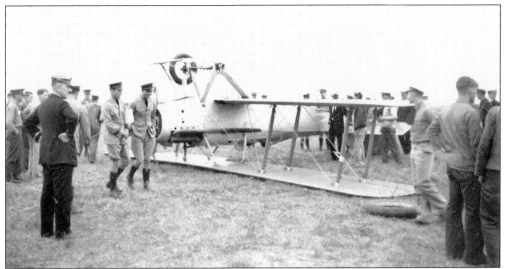

Accidents happen! Designed as a trainer for the army, the Vought VE-7 was adopted by the navy as its first fighter plane. This VE-7G has had a landing mishap at NAS North Island.

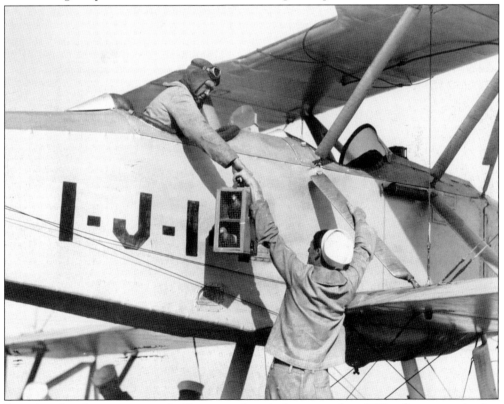

Even though radio receiving sets had been tested on airplanes as early as 1912, radio communication remained in its infancy during the 1920s. The radio sets of the time were heavy and unreliable, not at all well suited to use in the small spotter planes of the day. Carrier pigeons were still in use as a substitute, as shown in this 1927 photograph of a pair being handed up to the observer of one of squadron VJ-1F's Boeing NB-1 planes.

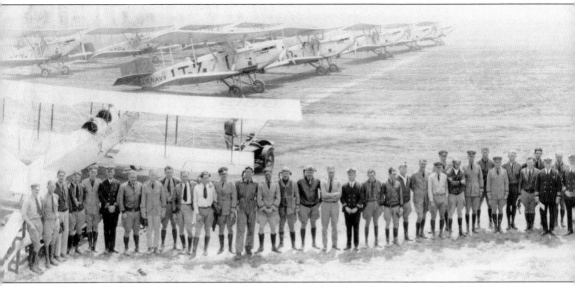

This wonderful panorama photograph was taken at Los Angeles in September 1928, just prior to the National Air Races. NAS San Diego was the primary home for West Coast naval aviation in the interwar years. Under the inspired direction of Rear Adm. Joseph M. Reeves, the base was aggressively involved in every available opportunity to get public attention and advance naval aviation in the public view. The *Langley* anchored off Manhattan Beach near the race site, and naval officials watched the flying from her deck. Standing in the center of the pilots is Rear

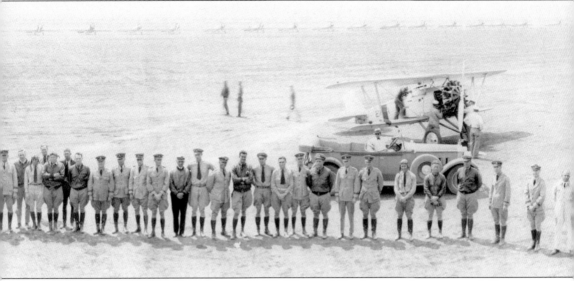

Admiral Reeves. Also present is Comdr. D. W. "Tommy" Tomlinson, whose personal Curtiss Jenny appears on the left. Tomlinson was the commanding officer of squadron VB-2B. Tomlinson was responsible for forming the navy's first aerial demonstration team in 1927. Known as "the Three Seahawks," this team was the true forefathers of today's famous Blue Angels. Later he was a vice president of TWA.

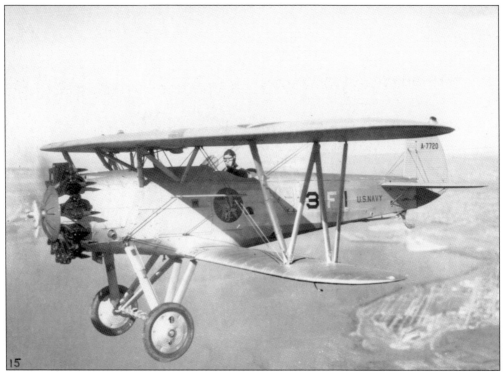

This beautifully posed photograph of a Boeing F3B-1 shows Lt. Comdr. S. P. Ginder, commanding officer of VF-3B, flying over San Diego. This fighter squadron was assigned to the USS *Saratoga* when this picture was taken in 1930. The F3B entered service in 1929 and was capable of speeds up to 157 miles per hour.

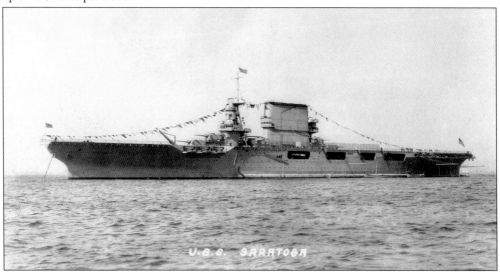

The USS *Saratoga* is dressed out for a presidential review between the wars. Both ships of this class were originally laid down as battle cruisers but were completed as America's first modern fleet carriers. *Saratoga* was commissioned in 1927 and survived the Second World War only to be sunk during postwar atomic bomb tests at Bikini Atoll in 1946. Also commissioned in 1927, the USS *Lexington* was sunk during the Battle of Coral Sea in May 1942.

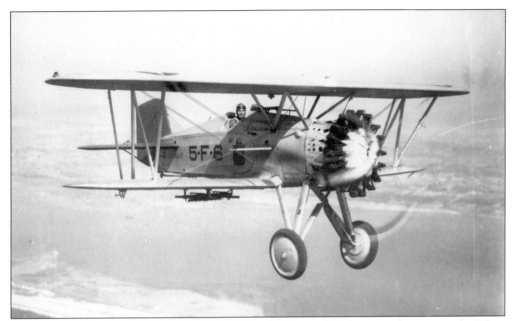

Assigned to the USS *Lexington* in 1930, this VF-5B Boeing F4B-1 is seen flying over the Silver Strand with San Diego Bay visible beyond. The F4B-1 was the first of the very popular F4B series that would remain in service until the eve of World War II. The big smile on the face of the pilot reflects most aviators' memories of flying the F4B. Note the practice bomb racks under the wing.

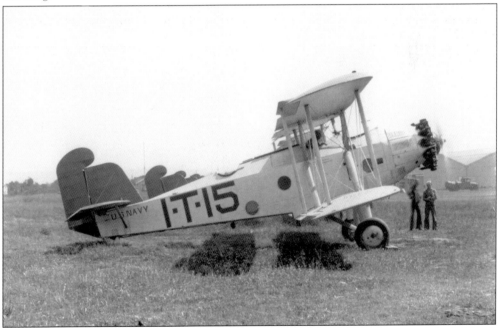

Also seen in 1930 is this Martin T4M-1 torpedo bomber from VT-1 on the grass at North Island. Martin built 102 of these large three-seaters for the navy, while the Great Lakes Company continued the production of an additional 50 as the TG-1 and TG-2. The lumbering type remained in frontline service until finally replaced by the Douglas TBD Devastator in 1935.

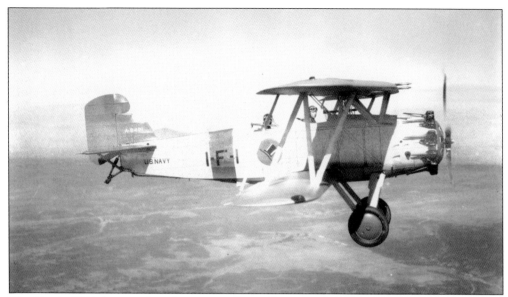

The Curtiss F8C-4 assigned to the commanding officer of Fighting Squadron 1 cruises over San Diego County in 1931. These two-seat planes were assigned to VF-1B on board the USS *Saratoga* and were only operated by the squadron for one year before being replaced by single-seat Boeing F4B-3s. The two photographs on this page are typical of J. M. F. Haase's photographic style. They are as much of the pilots and crew as they are of the airplanes and are truly evocative of naval aviation in the interwar period.

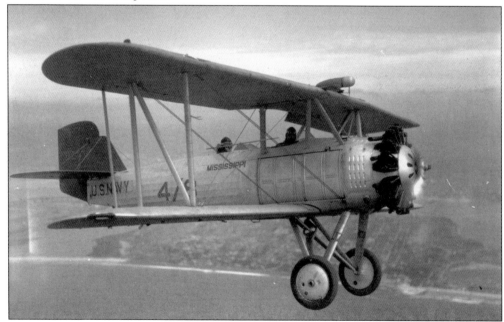

Seen here over the San Diego coastline in 1930 is a Vought O2U-1 assigned to VO-4B, aboard the USS *Mississippi*. The city of Coronado is directly behind the plane. The first of the famous Vought Corsairs, 130 production O2U-1 models were built. When the battleships and cruisers and carriers were in port at San Pedro, the planes were stored, maintained, or operated off wheeled gear at NAS North Island.

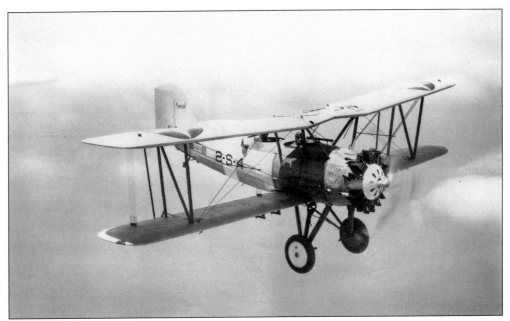

The Vought O2U-2 Corsair was used as a scout and spotting plane for the fleet. Various versions were in service from 1922 until they finally disappeared from service as trainers in the early 1940s. This aircraft is serving with VS-2B off the USS *Saratoga* in 1931 and is seen over Point Loma while flying out of NAS San Diego.

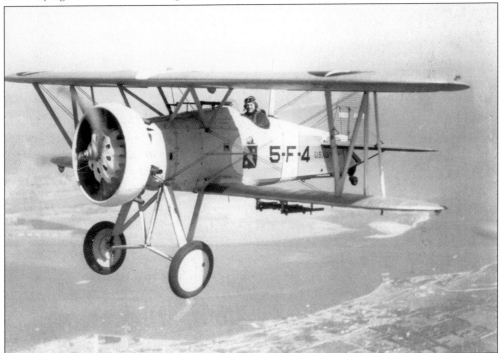

By 1931, Boeing had switched production from the first version of the F4B series, the F4B-1, to the F4B-2. This aircraft carried a cowling to reduce drag, improved landing gear and controls, and could carry a radio, as does this example. This plane is assigned to VF-5B off the USS *Lexington*.

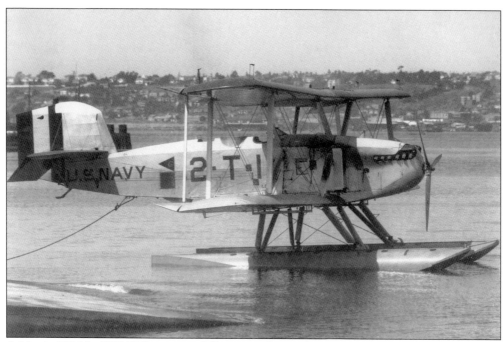

A Martin T3M-2 of VT-2B floats peacefully next to the seaplane ramp. These planes were operated on floats and fixed landing gear while at NAS North Island. This photograph was taken in 1927 or early 1928.

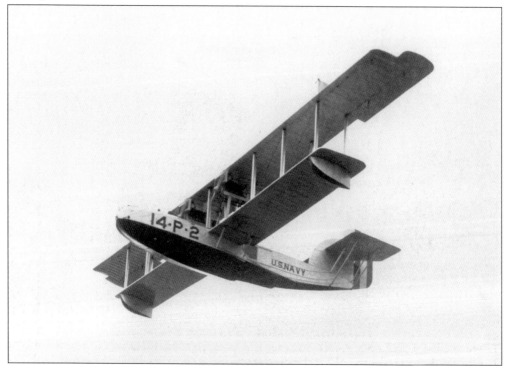

A Curtiss F5L cruises sedately over the photographer in 1928. This was late in the career for this World War I type, and most had left service by 1929. This plane is assigned to VP-14F as 14-P-2.

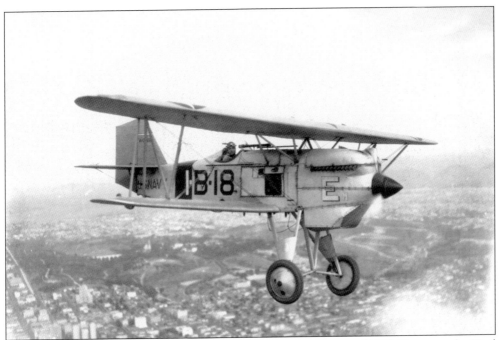

A Curtiss F6C-3 of VB-1B cruises over San Diego during the summer of 1928. Known as the "Red Rippers," the squadron had previously operated as VF-5S. Visible under the tail is famous Balboa Park, home of the San Diego Zoo.

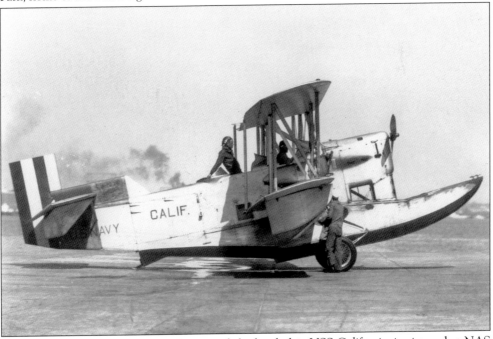

Loening OL-6, Bureau No. A-7336, assigned the battleship USS *California*, is pictured at NAS North Island *c.* 1927. The navy bought more than 80 various versions of this distinctive amphibian design. Powered by a 440-horsepower Packard engine, 28 of the three-place OL-6 "Flying Shoehorns" were acquired.

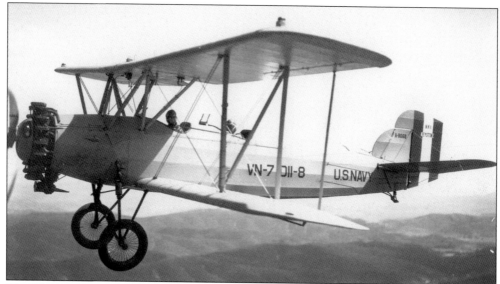

This Keystone NK-1 was assigned to the reserve squadron at NAS North Island. Built as a result of a 1928 competition for a new training aircraft for the fleet, the Keystone NK-1 was powered by a Wright R-790 engine. Nineteen were built. The reserves have always played an important role in naval aviation. Most major naval air stations hosted at least one unit. Naval reserve air bases were established near major population concentrations wherever there was not a large NAS.

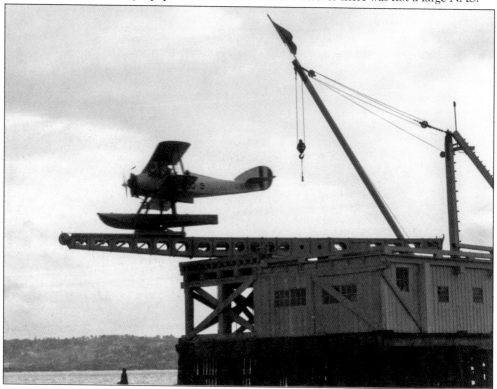

A Vought UO-1 of VJ-1 launches from a pier-mounted catapult at NAS North Island around 1928. The catapult was used for training pilots for the fleet for a number of years.

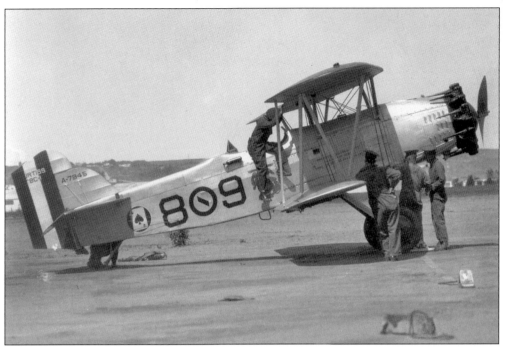

Originally ordered as two-seat fighters for the U.S. Marine Corps with the designation F8C-1, these planes were soon redesignated as OC-1 multipurpose aircraft. This photograph is of F8C-1 number A-7945, assigned to VO-8M, and was taken on the U.S. Marine Corps' ramp just two days after its delivery at NAS North Island in March 1928.

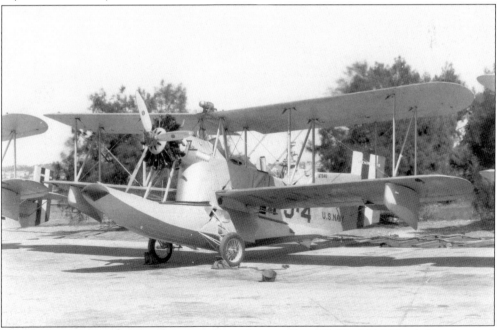

This Loening OL-8 amphibian is assigned to utility squadron VJ-1F at NAS North Island around 1928. The navy bought more than 80 various versions of this distinctive amphibian design. Twenty of the three-place, Pratt and Whitney Wasp–powered OL-8 version were acquired.

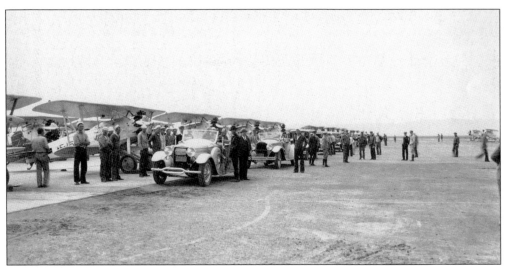

Popular among the fads of the 1920s were various cross-country events. Shown here at the start of one such trip is a line up of new cars visiting North Island. The lead vehicle is a 1929 Lincoln, followed by a 1929 Packard. The planes behind them are Boeing F2B-1 fighters assigned to VF-1B. Fighting Squadron 1 was assigned to the USS *Lexington* at the time.

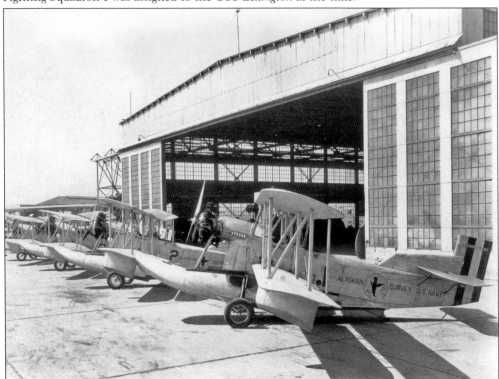

All of the Loening OL-8A amphibians assigned to the second Alaskan Aerial Survey are seen lined up in front of the utility hangar at NAS North Island in May 1929. Each plane in the unit was named for an Alaskan city. Aircraft 1, serial A-8072, was *Juneau*. The navy ordered 20 OL-8A amphibians, the first of the series to be equipped with arresting gear for carrier operations. J. M. F. Haase was the chief photographer for this project.

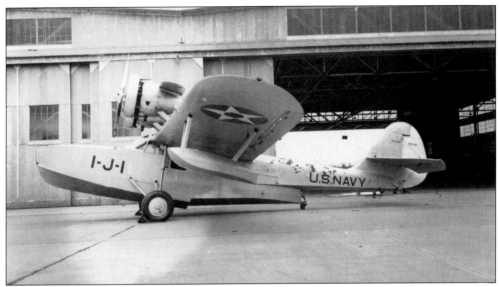

The navy acquired several of these versatile Douglas RD Dolphin amphibians in the 1930s. Most, like this one from VJ-1, were used by navy utility squadrons, but one was specially fitted out as a presidential transport for Franklin D. Roosevelt.

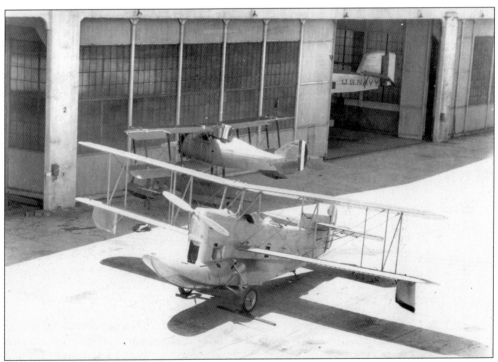

An early Loening OL, either an OL-1 or OL-3, sits in front of a hangar at NAS North Island. This distinctive type served in relatively large numbers with both the army and navy. This version is powered by a 440-horsepower Packard engine.

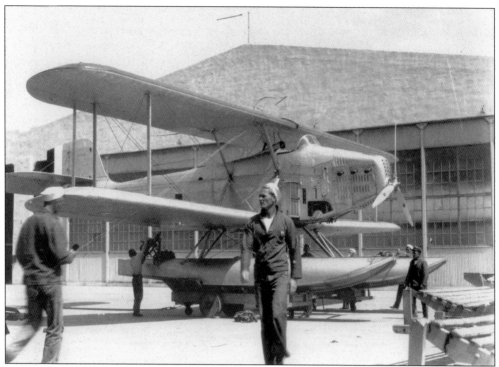

Boeing designed this airplane as a competitor to the Martin T3M-2. The two XTB-1s built were powered by a 730-horsepower Packard 1A-2500. Though the plane could be flown with floats or fixed landing gear, Boeing failed to win a contract, and the type did not enter series production.

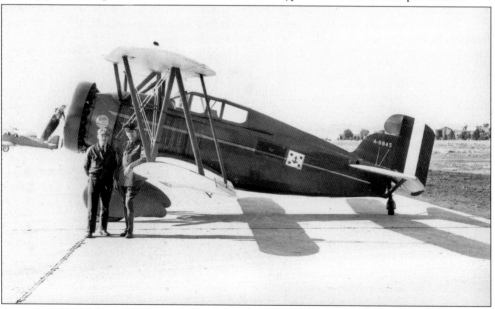

Curtiss XF8C-7, No. A-8845, was delivered as a staff plane for Secretary of the Navy David S. Ingalls. Painted gloss blue with gold trim and silver wings, the plane carries a placard on the fuselage displaying the symbol for the secretary of the navy. This photograph was taken at NAS San Diego in 1930.

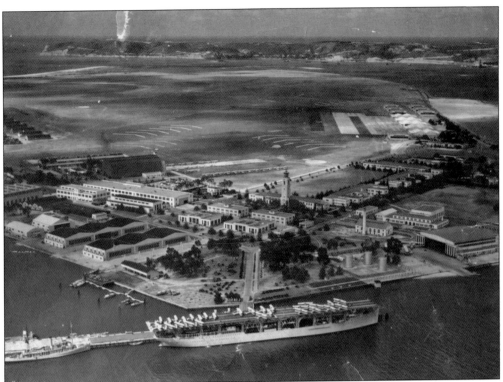

This is an aerial view of North Island looking southwest taken c. 1932. Tied up at the navy's pier are the USS *Langley* and a Bird-class small seaplane tender, likely the USS *Avocet*. *Langley* carried 32 planes at this time, and 28 of them appear on deck. At the time, all of the landing fields on the island were still dirt and grass, although some cement hardstands had finally appeared in front of the training and lighter-than-air hangars.

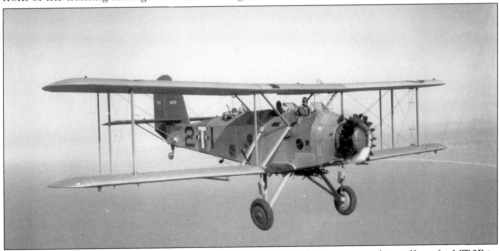

A Great Lakes TG-1 is pictured in the markings of the squadron commanding officer for VT-2B in 1931. The Great Lakes TG series of torpedo bombers came into being when Great Lakes acquired the Martin Company's Cleveland factory in 1928. The TG was the last of the U.S. Navy biplane torpedo bombers. The TG series lasted in service until 1937, when they were finally replaced by the monoplane Douglas TBD Devastator.

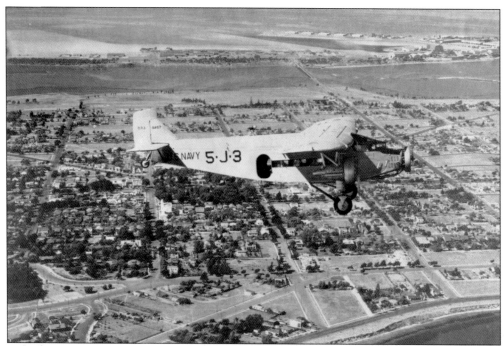

The navy carried out a very active parachute training program at NAS San Diego throughout the 1920s and 1930s. Most of the transport planes acquired for the fleet were basically civilian types modified for military needs. This Ford RR-3 trimotor assigned to Utility Squadron 5 is seen over Coronado with Spanish Bight, North Island, and Point Loma visible above the plane. Note that the door has been removed to facilitate the parachutists.

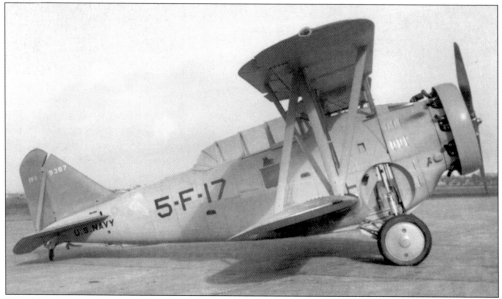

This blue-tailed Grumman FF-1 from VF-5B is seen on a cross-country flight out of NAS San Diego. The FF-1 was the navy's first production fighter to be equipped with drag-reducing retractable landing gear. VF-5B was the only squadron to be equipped with the Grumman, which flew off the USS *Lexington* from 1933 to 1935.

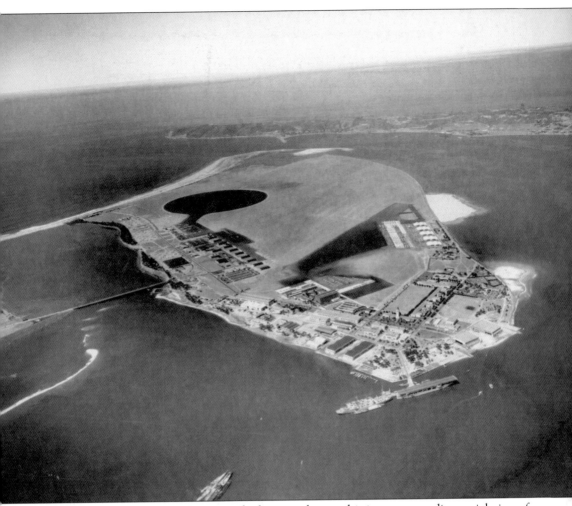

Taken from over the city of San Diego, looking southwest, this is an outstanding aerial view of North Island in 1933. At the time, North Island was still separated from Coronado by Spanish Bight and was only accessible via the causeway visible in the left center of the photograph. The various landing fields and taxiways were primarily dirt that was sprayed with oil to keep the dust under control. The circular army landing area can be seen in the center of the photograph, while the navy's landing area is to the right of center. The USS *Langley* can be seen tied up to the pier.

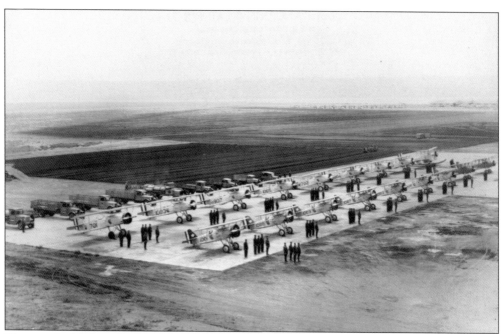

This wonderful photograph was taken sometime in mid-1931. It shows nearly the entire inventory of Marine West Coast Expeditionary Force San Diego lined up for a formal inspection on their newly completed hardstand. Visible are VF-10M's F6C-4 fighters, the OC-2 observation and attack planes, the single OL-8 utility plane assigned to VO-8M, the OC-2s assigned to VO-10M, the OC-1 and N2C-2 trainers of VJ-7M, and all of their assigned vehicles. Behind the ranked aircraft, tractors continue their work improving the field.

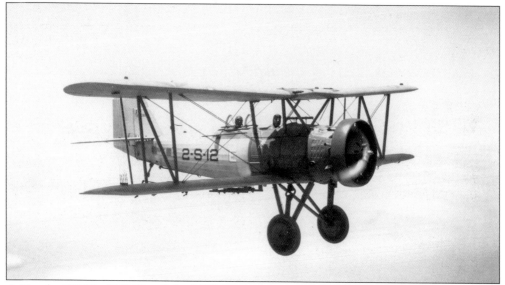

A Vought O2U-2 of VS-2B, off the USS *Saratoga*, soars over the San Diego coastline in 1930. A continuation of the famous Corsair series of observation planes, 37 Vought O2U-2 models were built in 1930, most serving initially with scouting squadrons VS-2B and VS-3B on the USS *Saratoga* and USS *Lexington*. Some also served with VO-1B as battleship scouts on floats, and six were diverted to the Coast Guard.

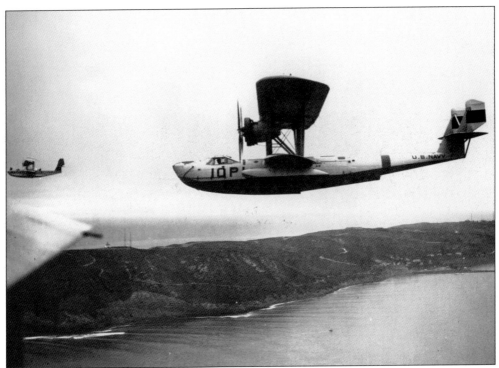

Six Consolidated P2Y-1 seaplanes of Patrol Squadron 10, under the command of Lt. Comdr. K. McGinnis, are seen over Point Loma after leaving their North Island base for San Francisco in early January 1934. On January 10, they flew nonstop from San Francisco to Pearl Harbor, Hawaii—2,399 miles in 24 hours 56 minutes, faster than any previous passage and a record for a formation of C-class flying boats.

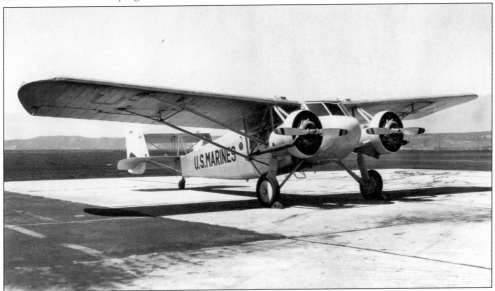

This Curtiss RC-1 Kingbird was among the many one-off types acquired by the navy and marines during the 1930s. Operated by the marines from North Island primarily as a staff transport with Marine Utility Squadron 7, the Kingbird became a familiar sight at West Coast airports.

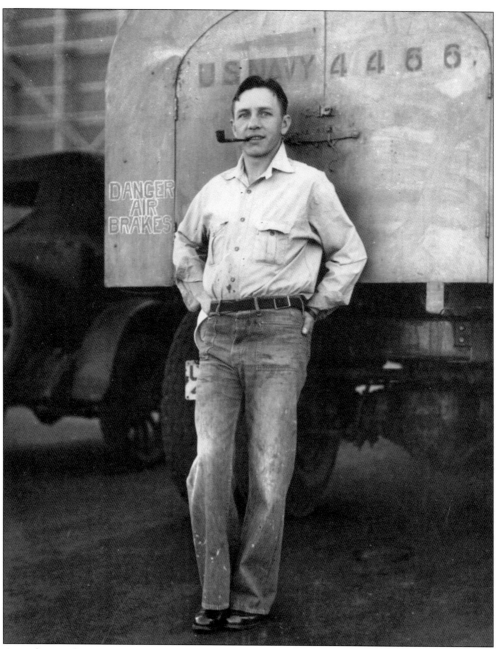

A professional sailor enjoys a pipe while leaning against the back of a navy truck at North Island in the 1920s. The navy offered a decent living, travel, and training not readily available elsewhere during the difficult years of the Depression.

Four

VISITORS FROM THE CIVILIAN WORLD
1927–1941

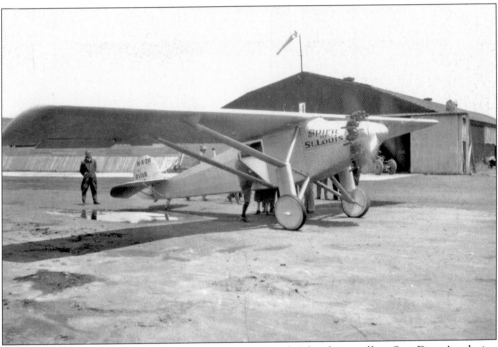

The relatively sophisticated facilities offered on North Island, as well as San Diego's relative location as the farthest southwest point in the country, led many interesting and historic aircraft and flyers to visit or use it as a beginning or terminus for distance flights. The following chapter will document many of the civilian visitors to the military world. By the late 1930s, the number of civilian aircraft visiting the base rapidly diminished as the need for security increased. Probably the most famous civilian airplane to visit North Island is seen on the ramp at Rockwell Field in late April 1927. This is Charles Lindbergh's *Spirit of St. Louis*, in which he captured the famous Orteig Prize just about three weeks later. Lindbergh began the first leg of his historic flight from North Island on May 9, 1927.

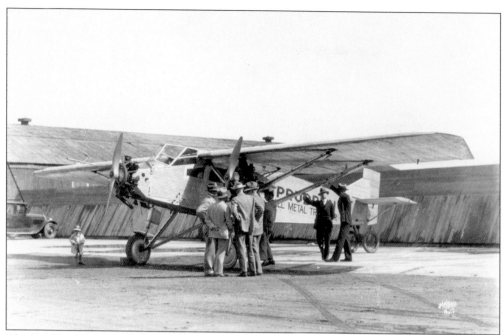

The Prudden TM-1 trimotor, seen here at NAS North Island in 1928, was powered by three 125-horsepower Siemens-Halske SH-12 engines. While this design was not successful, the company went on to become Solar Aircraft Company, which is still based in San Diego today.

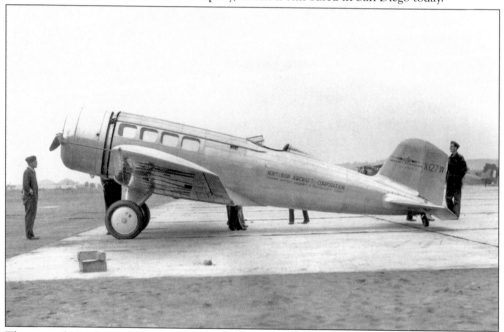

The second Northrop Alpha 2, X-127, sits on the ramp at NAS North Island. The plane was later modified to an Alpha 4 and sold to TWA. The first of Jack Northrop's high-performance transports, the Alpha was an all-metal, low-wing monoplane in a day when the fabric-covered biplane ruled the skies. Powered by a 420-horsepower Pratt and Whiney Wasp, the plane was carefully cowled and streamlined.

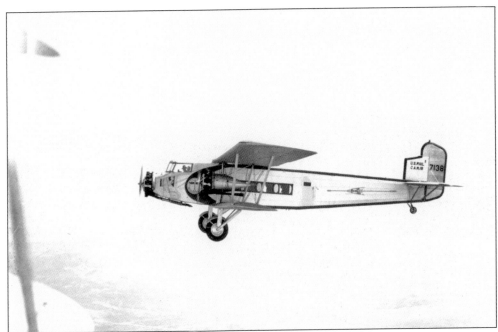

A Boeing Model 80, registered C7138, of Boeing Air Transport is pictured over San Diego during a visit to the NAS around 1929. The last of four built, these planes were used on the San Francisco–Chicago route.

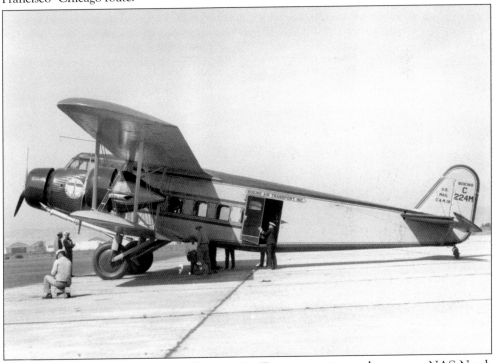

Boeing Model 80A, No. C-224M, of Boeing Air Transport waits on the ramp at NAS North Island c. 1930. Painted gloss gray with Boeing green trim and orange wing tops, these planes were very colorful.

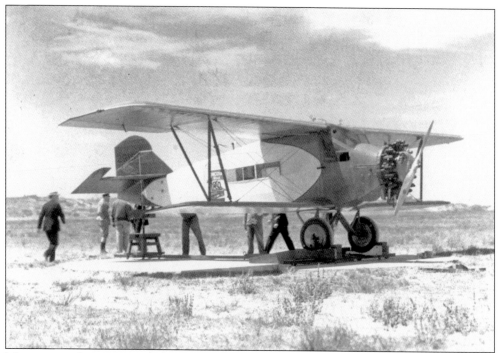

Many new and experimental planes were flown to NAS North Island to have their instruments calibrated by the navy. This photograph shows Buhl CA-5, No. C-2915, being readied for the Dole Race in August 1927. Flown by J. Pedlar with V. Knope as navigator and schoolteacher Mildred Doran as a crewmember, the plane departed Oakland for Hawaii on August 16. They were lost at sea and never heard from again.

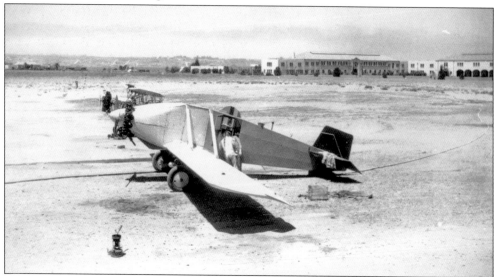

The curious-looking Tremaine Humming Bird at NAS North Island has its instruments checked prior to the Dole Race. The plane was named *Spirit of John Rodgers* for the race and was flown by Lt. George D. Covell, age 28, with Lt. Richard S. Waggener as navigator. Sadly on August 10, 1927, both men perished shortly after takeoff from North Island when they flew into a cliff on Point Loma in foggy weather.

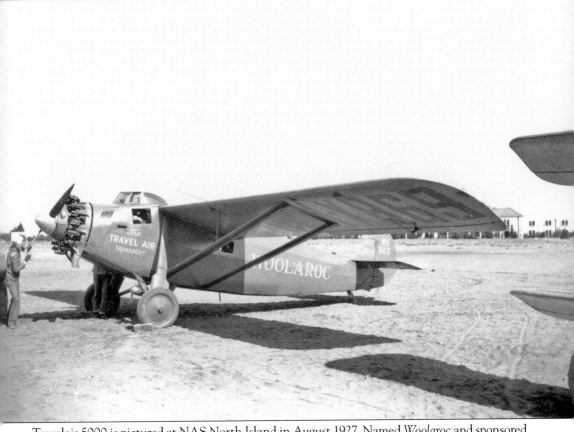

Travelair 5000 is pictured at NAS North Island in August 1927. Named *Woolaroc* and sponsored by Phillips Petroleum, the plane was specially modified for the August 1927 air race from Oakland to Honolulu. *Woolaroc* was the winning entry in the race and was piloted by Art Goebel; his navigator was Lt. William V. Davis Jr. of the U.S. Navy. The plane is currently preserved at the Woolaroc Museum in Bartlesville, Oklahoma.

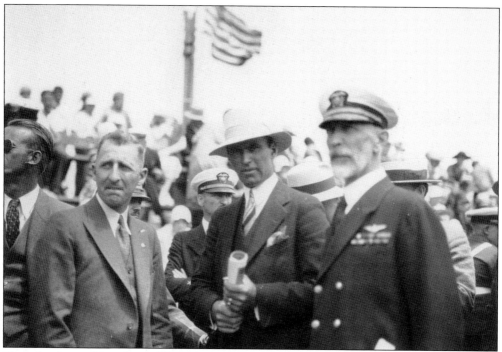

Goebel, a big and handsome World War I flier, is seen with Admiral Reeves at the 1928 Los Angeles air races, a year after his record-setting flight to Hawaii.

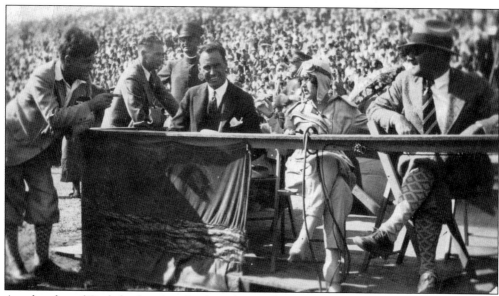

Another shot of Goebel at Los Angeles shows him with famous aviatrix Ruth Elder. The celebrities of aviation during the 1920s and 1930s were a colorful group. Goebel had been a member of the "Thirteen Black Cats of Hollywood" stunt group. Elder was the first woman to attempt a transatlantic flight.

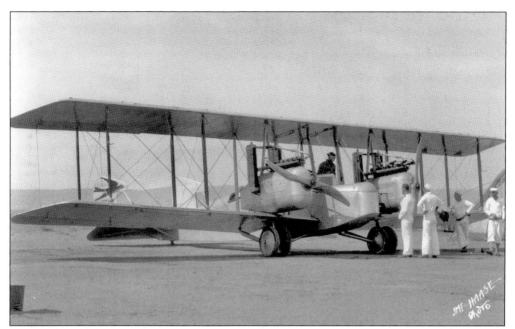

The Timm Skylark is inspected by curious sailors on the ramp at NAS North Island. This airplane was originally built by the Pacific Airplane and Supply Company of Venice, California, with a Curtiss OX-5 engine but was re-engined with two 200-horsepower Hall-Scott L-6 engines. It was later modified again by Otto Timm, as seen here with two Liberty engines.

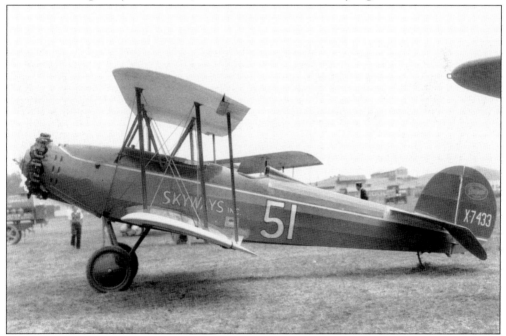

The prototype of the Kreider-Reisner C-5 series is seen on North Island's ramp in 1929. The name Challenger appears on the tail, and although the company downplayed that as the proper name for the type, it seems to have stuck with the machine. Three were built, all in 1929. The plane was powered by a Warner Scarab engine.

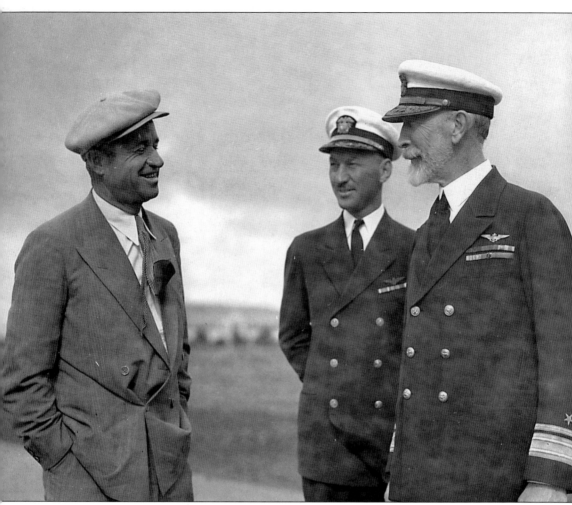

Many media luminaries also visited North Island, especially those with an interest in aviation. Famous humorist Will Rogers is seen here with Admiral Reeves. Rogers, already bitten by the aviation bug, was taken up for a ride in a flying boat.

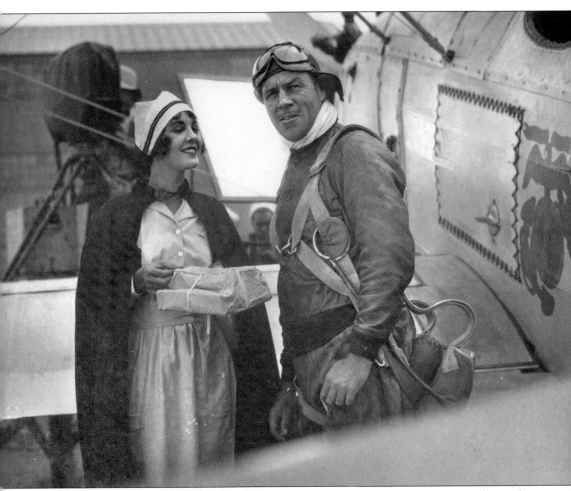

Because of the public's infatuation with aviation and North Island's relative proximity to Hollywood, the base became a familiar backdrop for many interwar movies. In this photograph, actors Lila Lee and Jack Holt are seen on the set of the 1929 movie *Flight*.

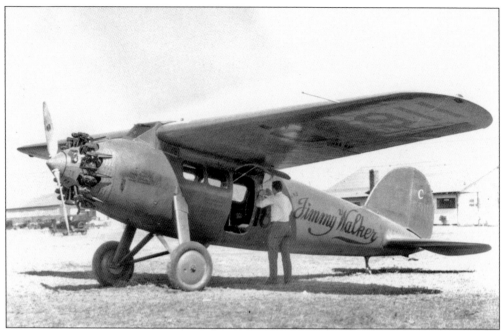

Seen shortly after arrival at North Island at the end of the 1928 National Air Races, Lockheed Vega number NX6911 was piloted by Bryan Shaw, taking 11th place in the Class B division. This aircraft would later be owned by Amelia Earhart. The famous type was designed by Jack Northrop, and the first plane was built in a rented building in Hollywood, California. Shortly thereafter, the company moved to Burbank.

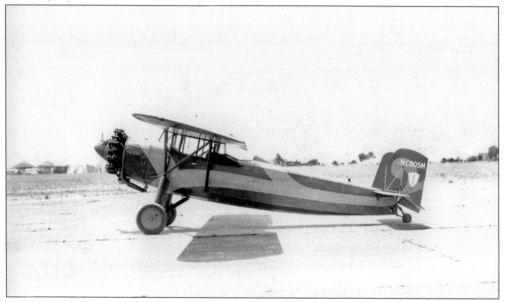

The graceful M-1 Parasol two-place monoplanes were built by the Moreland Aircraft, Inc., at Mines Field in El Segundo, California. They were powered by 220-horsepower Wright J-5 engines. Designed primarily for the use by businessmen, the market never developed, and only four were built. This particular machine was still in use in 1936 as a crop duster in the banana plantations of Central America.

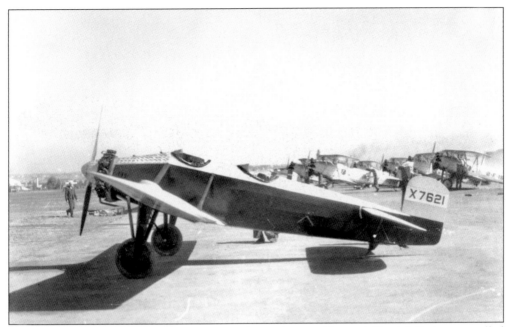

The Mahoney-Ryan X-1 Sportster was an experimental type with a variable-airfoil wing controlled by a lever in the cockpit. The airplane had no fixed fin or stabilizer, which were replaced by a large moveable "stabilator" and rudder. The fuselage had an adjustable 50-pound weight on a track to shift the center of gravity.

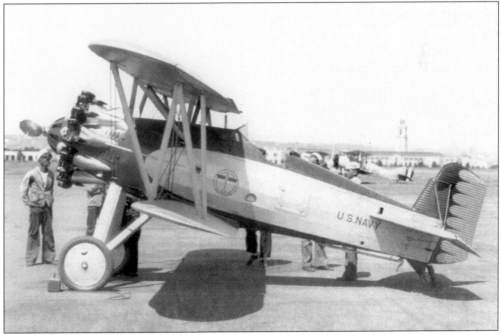

Built as a private venture by the Boeing Company in Seattle, the Model 83 was the prototype for the navy's famous F4B series as well as the army's P-12. Pictured on the ramp at NAS North Island in 1928, the target of Boeing's marketing effort is certainly made clear by the tailhook under the aft fuselage.

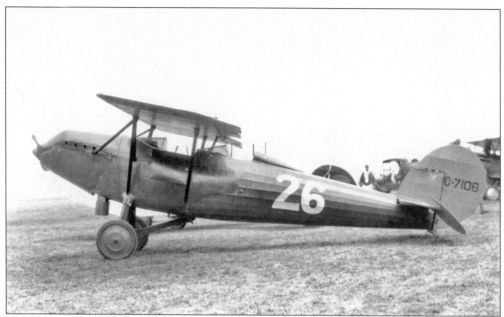

This interesting-looking monoplane is a Berliner CM-4. Powered by the famous OX-5 engine, the CM-4 was the first parasol to earn an Air Transport Certificate (ATC). Six were built in 1928. The Berliner Company went on to become Berliner-Joyce.

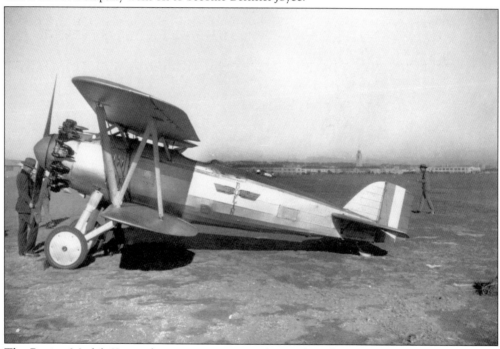

The Boeing Model 69, another private venture advanced to the navy in hopes of a contract, was to become the prototype of the F2B series of navy fighters. During testing, the navy gave it the designation XF2B-1, making it one of the very first planes to carry an X (experimental) designation. Seen here on the flight line at NAS North Island in 1926, the airplane carries the green Boeing totem logo on the fuselage.

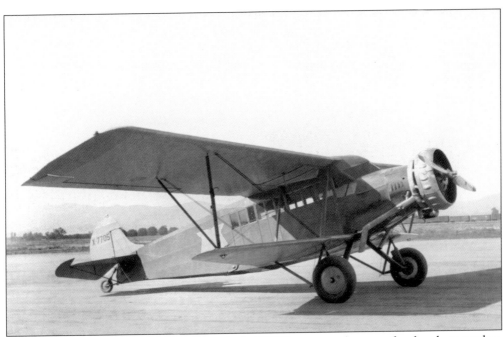

One of two Buhl CA-8 Senior Airsedans built, X7705 poses on the ramp for the photographer. Powered by a 450-horsepower Pratt and Whitney Wasp, only two of these interesting-looking sesquiplanes were built. A variation of the biplane was the sesquiplane, where the (usually) lower wing was significantly smaller than the other, either in span, chord, or both. On occasion, the lower wing was only large enough to support the bracing struts for the upper wing. The name means "one-and-a-half wings."

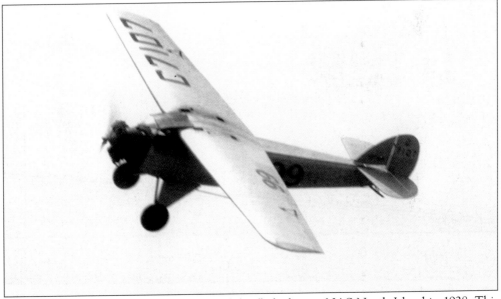

Cessna AW No. C7107 performs a flyby of the flight line at NAS North Island in 1928. This was the first AW of 58 built, and it won the New York-to-Los Angeles Air Derby in 1928 flown by Earl Rowland. Powered by the 110-horsepower Warner Scarab engine, they cost about $7,000 new and had a range of about 630 miles.

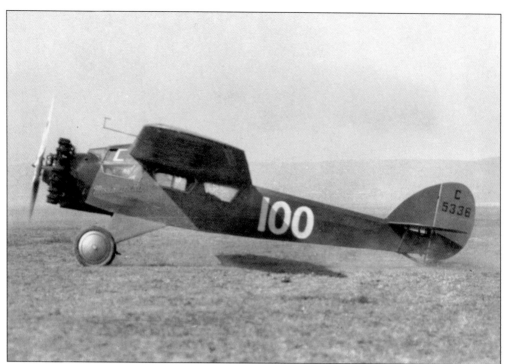

This Cessna BW was registered as C-5336. This sleek-looking airplane carried race number 100. Built as a "sportsman" version of the Cessna AW and powered by a 220-horsepower Wright J-5, 12 of these four-place planes were built, but because of Department of Commerce rules regarding certification, only three seats were fitted.

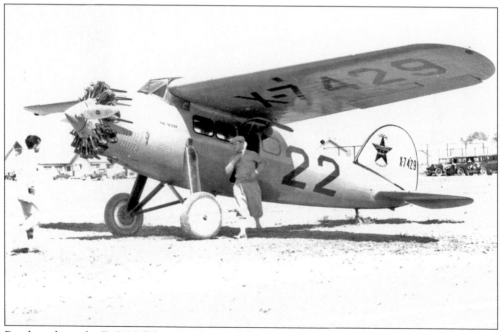

Purchased new by E. P. Halliburton, this Lockheed Vega 5, registered X7429, was a competitor in the 1928 National Air Race.

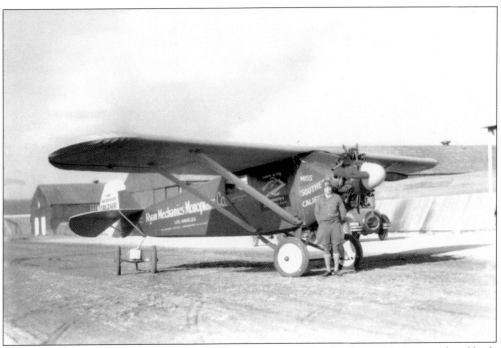

Ryan Mechanics CM-1 No. NX4041 is pictured at NAS North Island in 1928. Designed and built at Vail Field by three former Ryan employees, the plane embodied characteristics of the Ryan Brougham and the Waterhouse Cruzair.

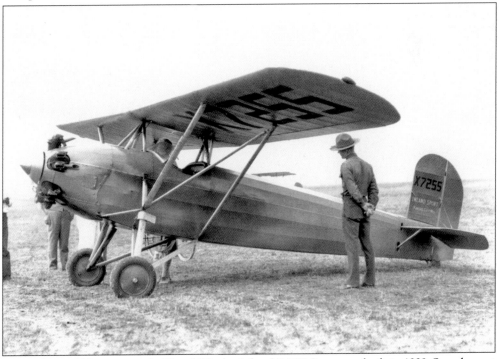

Powered by a 65-horsepower LeBlond 5D, the Inland S-300 Sport was built in 1929. Seen here at Rockwell Field, this is the prototype for the 17 built.

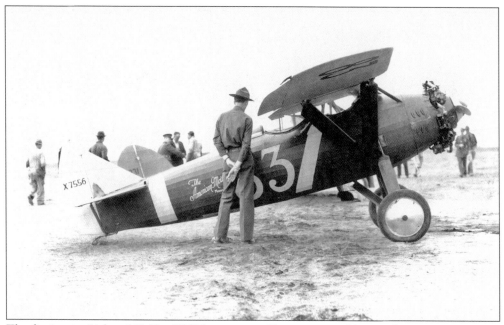

The diminutive Vulcan V-1, No. C7556, is inspected by a curious soldier on the ramp at NAS San Diego in 1927. Also known as the American Moth, the plane was powered by a 60-horsepower Detroit Air Cat engine.

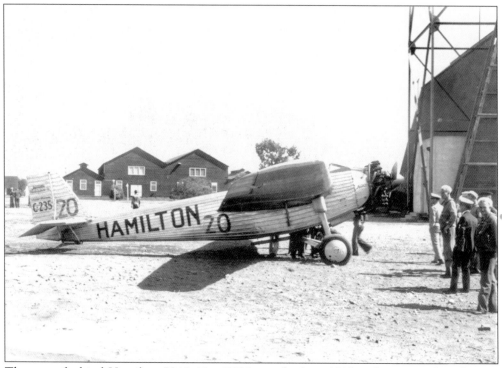

The one-of-a-kind Hamilton H-18, No. C235, was built in 1927 and competed in the Air Tour that year, taking second place as *Maiden Milwaukee*. It was the first all-metal plane to be licensed in the U.S.

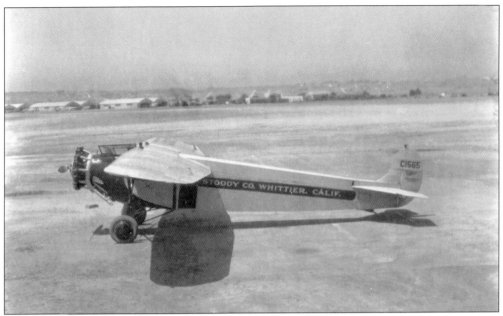

Eighty of these sturdy Fokker Super Universals were built by Fokkers' American subsidiary while others were built under license in Japan and Canada. Seen at North Island in 1929, this airplane was registered as C1565 to the Stoody Company of Whittier, California.

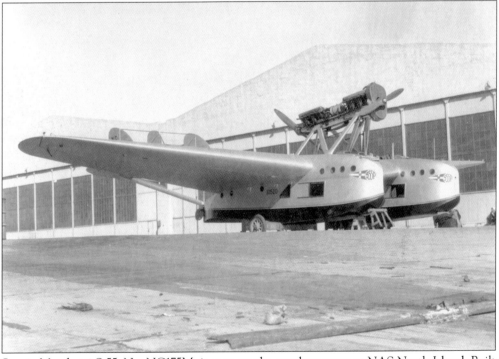

Savoia-Marchetti S-55, No. NC175M, is seen on the seaplane ramp at NAS North Island. Built under license by the American Aeronautical Company, the Savoia planes made in this country were generally referred to as "American Marchettis" to conceal their Italian origin. Three S-55s were built at a factory in Port Washington, New York.

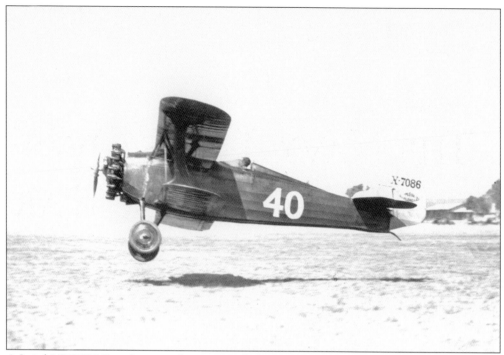

A Laird LC-R200 Speedwing is about to touch down at NAS San Diego in 1929. Five of these graceful Wright J-5–powered custom two-seaters were built. Note the streamlined I struts.

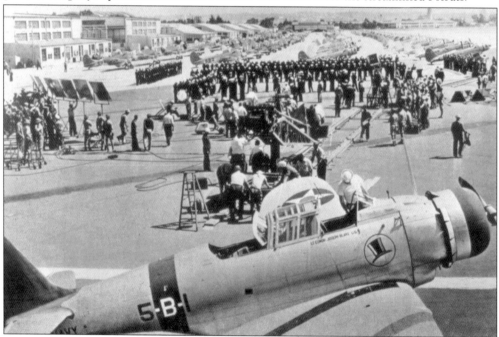

Another well-known aviation movie filmed on the North Island ramp was 1941's *Dive Bomber*. Starring Errol Flynn, Ralph Bellamy, and Fred McMurray, the movie was filmed in Technicolor and clearly showed the popular shift away from isolationism as war approached. This view was taken on the ramp at the base during the filming of the movie's last scene.

Five

THE NAVY TAKES OVER AND PREPARES FOR WAR
1935–1941

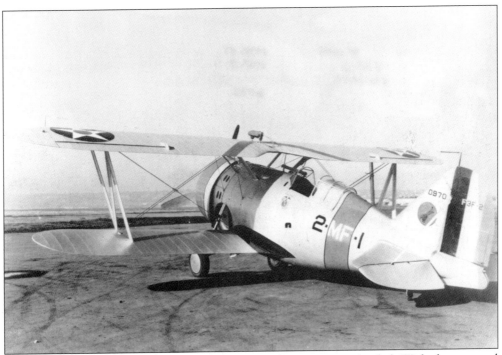

By the mid-1930s operations at North Island were becoming overloaded. With the personal approval of Pres. Franklin D. Roosevelt, the army officially turned Rockwell Filed over to the navy on October 25, 1935. During this period, aviation really began to come of age, and the U.S. Navy at North Island was at the forefront in the development of aviation engineering, medicine, and technique. By 1939, international tensions had flared into war, and the United States began to prepare for its potential involvement in the conflict. This final chapter will examine the many new aircraft types and tactics, some of which would be destined to play a pivotal role in the coming conflict. A Grumman F3F-2 assigned to VMF-4 stands before the hangars on the ramp at NAS San Diego in 1937.

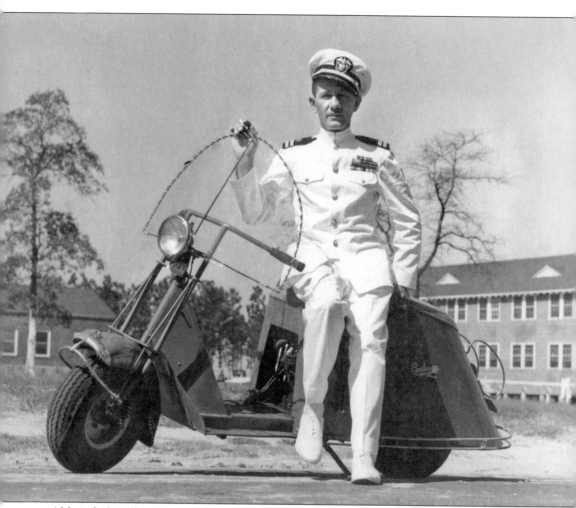

Although the officer in this undated photograph is not identified, his confidence and experience truly radiate in this photograph from the late 1930s.

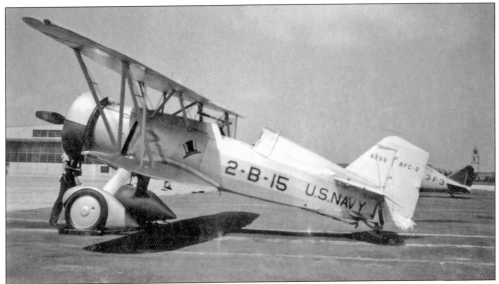

The attractive Curtiss Hawk series served the navy well during the interwar period. This aircraft is a BFC-2 fighter bomber from VB-2B and is seen on North Island's ramp in 1936. Assigned to the USS *Saratoga*, the BFC was replaced by the more modern Grumman F3F in 1938.

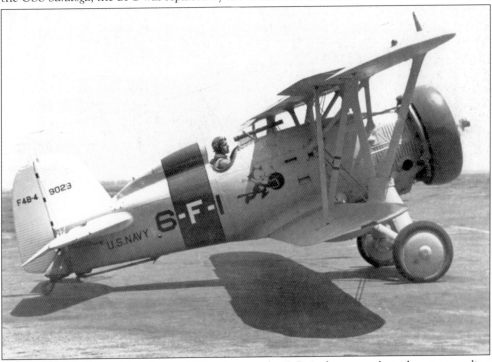

The ultimate version of the Boeing F4B series was the F4B-4; this example is the commanding officer's aircraft from VF-6B in 1936. Boeing owes their subsequent success in a large part to the F4B/P-12 series, which was extremely popular and reliable, leading to large orders from the army and navy, as well as some export orders. Ninety-two F4B-4s were delivered between April 1931 and February 1933. They ended their days as trainers and radio-controlled target drones in the early 1940s.

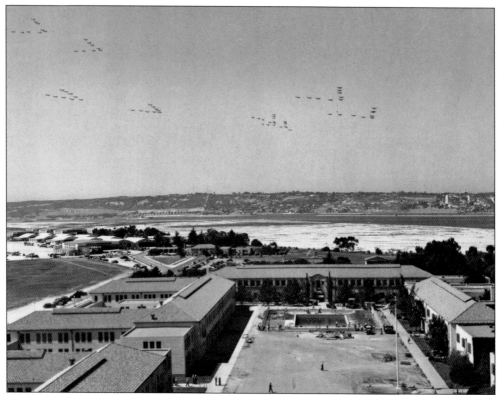

This is the view looking west from the control tower atop the base administration building *c.* 1936. Visible in the distance is Point Loma. The buildings in the foreground are mainly barracks, with a new swimming pool taking shape in the courtyard. Just beyond to the left are the fleet hangars, while overhead the sky is alive with dive and torpedo bombers and fighter planes.

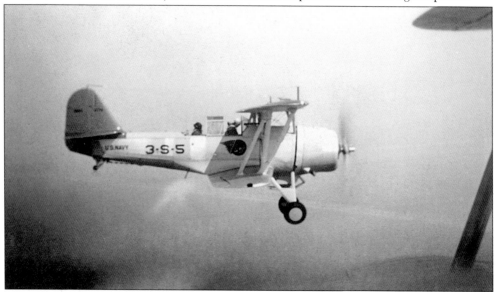

The Vought SBU was a scout bomber that finally provided some protection for the crew in the form of a partial canopy. VS-3 was operating the sturdy aircraft from the USS *Lexington* in 1937.

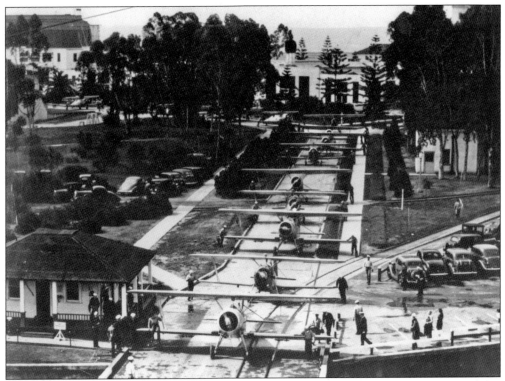

This undated photograph shows how carrier planes at North Island were delivered to their aircraft carriers for loading. They were simply taxied down the streets of the base to the dock, then loaded aboard by crane. The aircraft in the foreground are Vought SBU scout bombers, while Grumman F3F-2 fighters are in the rear.

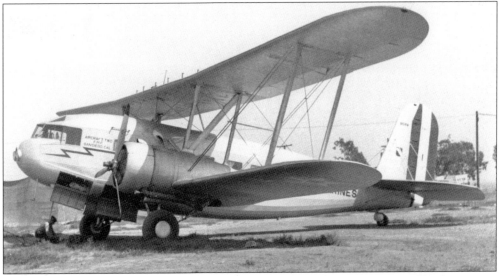

Delivered to the navy in 1934, two of these Curtiss AT-32E transports were operated by the marines as R4C-1s. Both were operated at NAS San Diego on North Island for about five years before being assigned to the U.S. Antarctic Service Expedition in 1939. This aircraft, Bureau No. 9854, was abandoned in Antarctica in 1941 and is presumed to be there still, buried under the snow.

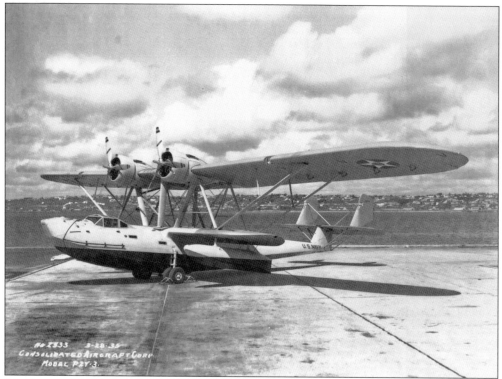

The first production Consolidated P2Y-3 was photographed at North Island on March 28, 1935. These airplanes were built at Consolidated's factory in Buffalo, New York, test flown from the Hudson River, and then delivered to the fleet. A year after this photograph was taken, Reuben Fleet, the president of Consolidated, would move the factory to San Diego, where the excellent weather allowed the production of flying boats year-round.

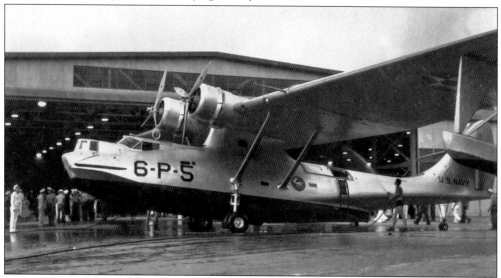

A Consolidated PBY-1 assigned to VP-6F prepares to launch into the harbor from NAS San Diego's seaplane ramp in 1937. The navy procured 60 of these modern flying boats for both patrol and bombing missions. It was a huge production order by contemporary standards.

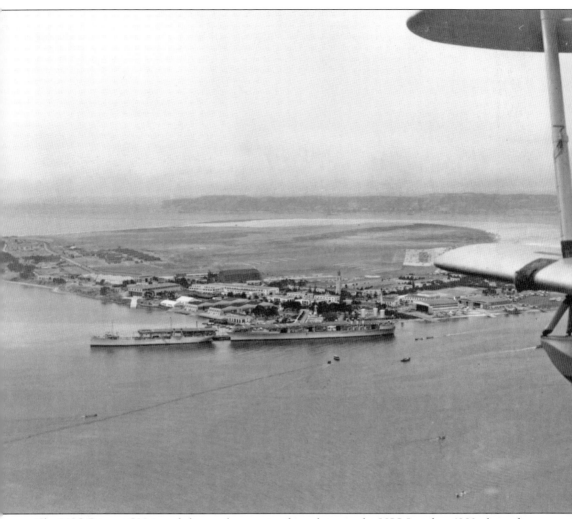

The USS *Ranger*, CV-4, and the newly converted seaplane tender USS *Langley*, AV-3, share the pier at NAS San Diego in 1937. *Ranger* was the first American ship to be built as an aircraft carrier from the keel up. Her six funnels were hinged to lie flat during aircraft operations. *Langley*, having outlived her usefulness as an aircraft carrier, was modified into a seaplane tender. She would serve in this guise until sunk by the Japanese in the Java Sea in February 1942.

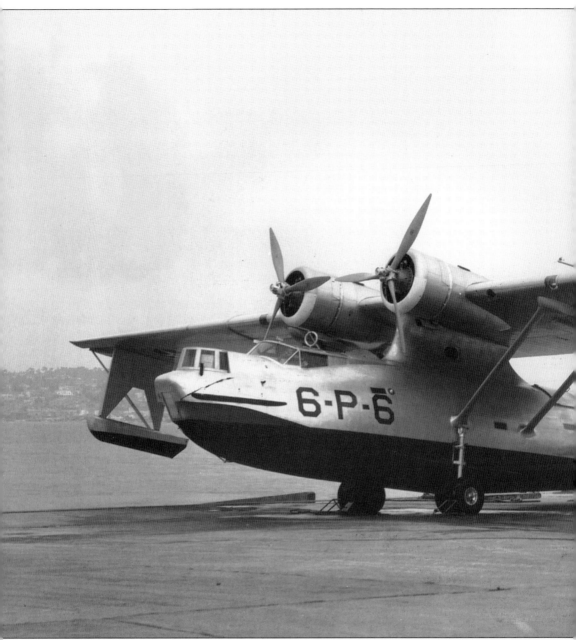

The first production PBY-1 Catalina shares the North Island seaplane ramp with the biplanes it would soon replace. The first squadron to receive the type was VP-6F. This photograph was taken on October 22, 1936. Powered by two Pratt and Whitney radial engines, the PBY could cruise

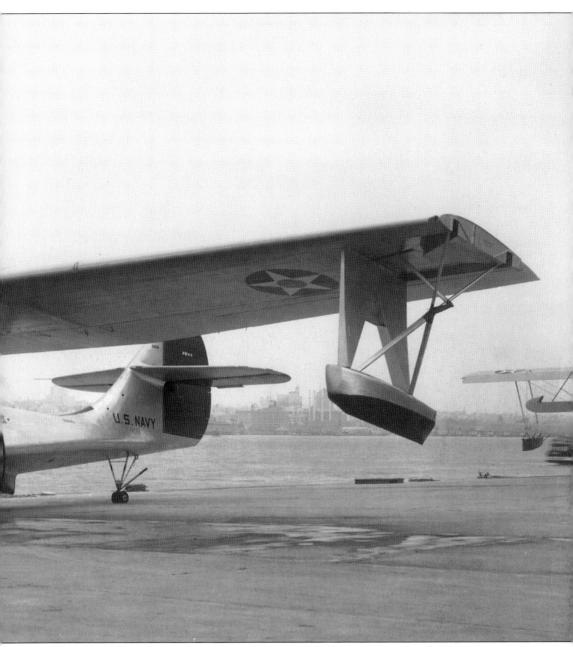

at 103 miles per hour for nearly twice the distance of the biplanes it replaced. Wartime versions sported large glass blisters on the fuselage sites to facilitate observation and gunnery.

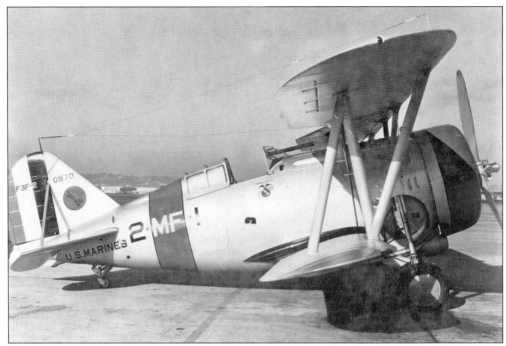

The last biplane fighter to serve with the U.S. Navy was the Grumman F3F-2. Seen here in the markings of Marine Fighting Squadron 2 is the commanding officer's airplane basking in San Diego's famous sunshine.

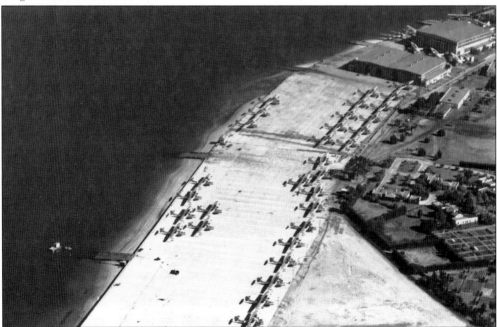

This aerial view of the seaplane parking area on the north end of the island was taken in 1937. There are at least 31 PBY seaplanes visible on the ramp. As the navy procured more modern aircraft during the military buildup of the late 1930s, there was a corresponding level of improvement in aircraft parking and maintenance facilities.

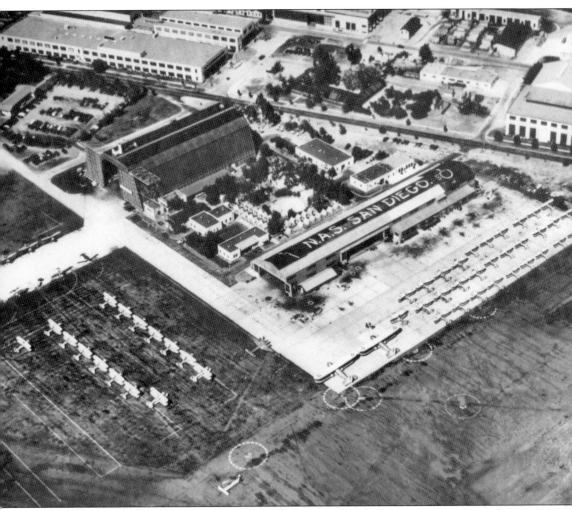

By the time this January 1939 photograph was taken, most of the parking areas and runways at North Island had been paved. Visible in this photograph are nearly all of the 60 U.S. Marine Corps aircraft then based at North Island with Fleet Marine Force, Aircraft 2. Among those that can be made out are two Curtiss R4C-1 Condor transports and a Lockheed JO-2 staff plane.

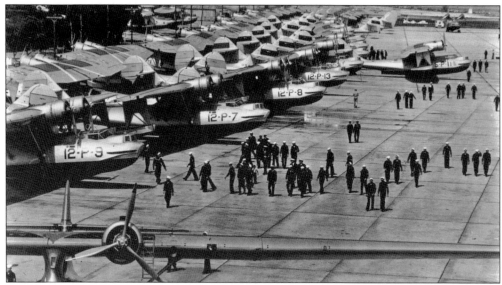

NAS San Diego's busy seaplane ramp is dominated by various models of early PBY Catalina flying boats in 1938. With the preservation of neutrality a major goal at the time, the navy had more PBY patrol planes in service than any other type. Visible in the photograph are aircraft from at least three squadrons.

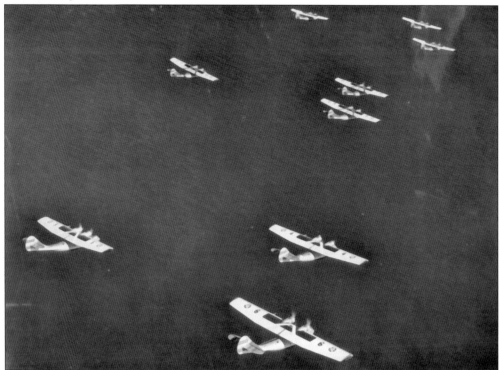

After the arrival of the legendary Catalina, the navy flew many long-distance formation flights using the Catalina. Competition for their share of the War Department's budget meant getting the attention of the American public. This photograph shows VP-11F preparing for such a flight from NAS San Diego to Fleet Air Base Coco Solo in the Panama Canal Zone in December 1938.

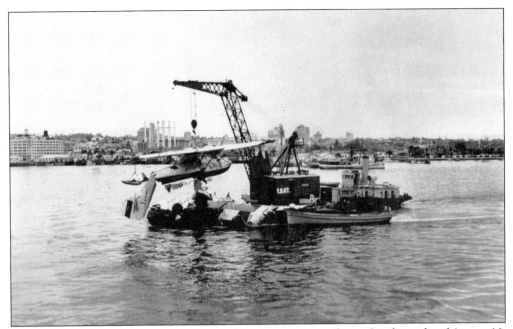

Increased levels of activity led to an inevitable increase in accidents. On the night of August 16, 1938, a formation landing led to a collision between two PBY-3 aircraft of VP-5 on San Diego Bay near National City. Four airmen were killed in the accident. This photograph shows the remains of the two aircraft being returned to NAS San Diego after salvage.

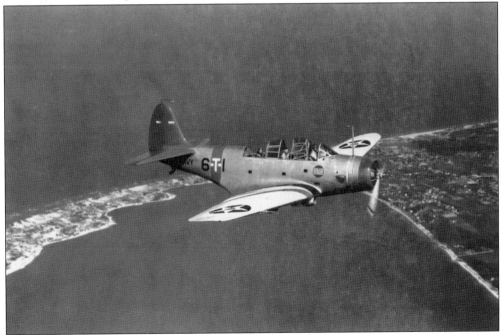

Epitomizing the transition from fabric-covered biplane to all-metal monoplane, the Douglas TBD Devastator torpedo bomber was introduced to the fleet in 1937 and replaced the venerable Great Lakes TG, which, in one form or another, had been in continuous service since the mid-1920s. This aircraft is the commanding officer's plane from VT-6 off the USS Enterprise.

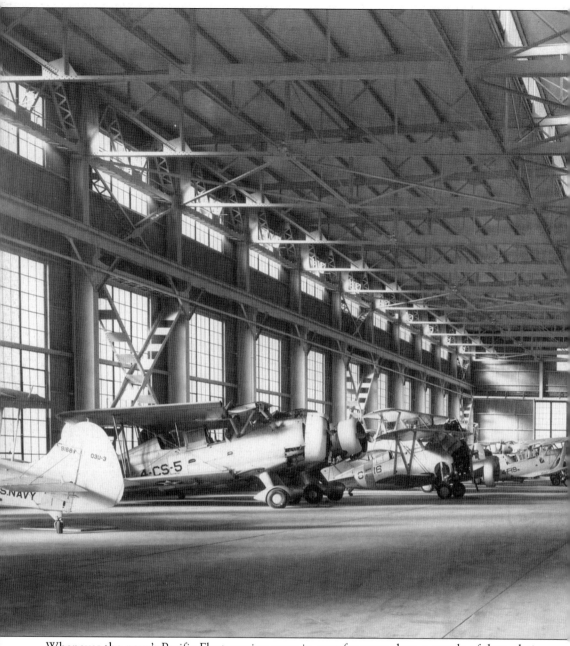

Whenever the navy's Pacific Fleet carriers were in port for more than a couple of days, their aircraft were flown off and serviced at North Island. This photograph was taken inside one of the base's maintenance hangars in 1940 and shows a truly remarkable selection of types then in service. Visible are Vought O3U and Curtiss SOC observation planes; Grumman FF and F3F-2

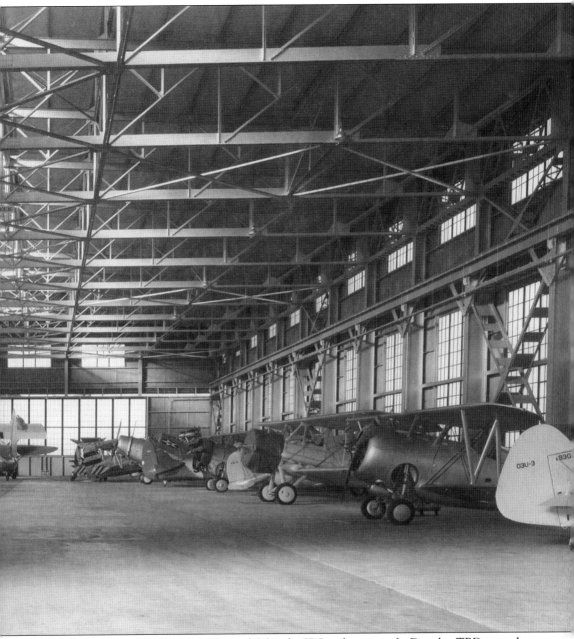

fighters; Grumman J2F, Douglas RD, and Sikorsky JRS utility aircraft; Douglas TBD torpedo bombers; and a Curtiss SBC-3 dive-bomber. Aircraft from at least three aircraft carriers and two cruisers are represented.

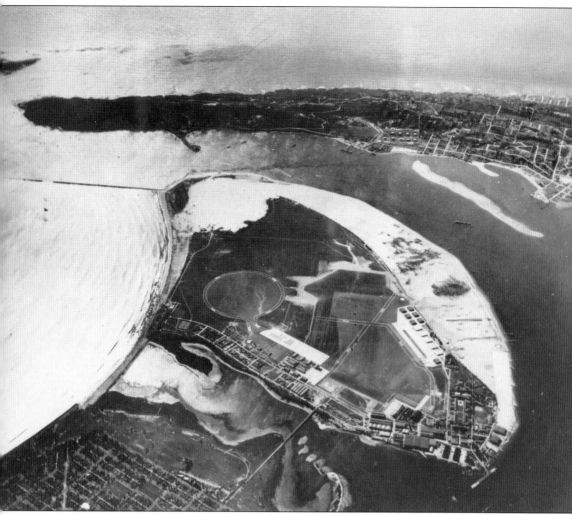

By 1939, the island was beginning to take on a different shape. Constant dredging of the bottom had added over 50 acres of land to the north and west sides. New seaplane ramps and hangars were built on the northern shoreline to accommodate the growing fleet of PBY patrol planes.

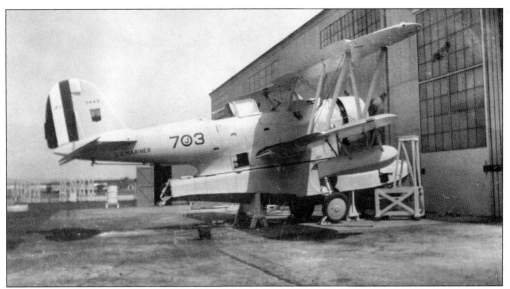

The Grumman Duck series was introduced into navy squadron service starting in 1936. The highly versatile utility type had a remarkably long career, not leaving regular service until well after World War II. This particular airplane is a JF-1 and is typical of the first production variant. It carries the markings of Marine Utility Squadron 7.

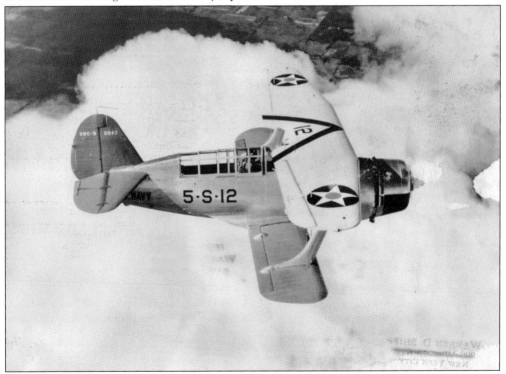

The Curtiss SBC brought the biplane combat aircraft era to an end for the navy. Introduced in 1937, the last marine planes with combat squadrons were not replaced by more modern types until 1942. Seen on a flight from NAS San Diego, this aircraft is assigned to VS-5 from the USS *Yorktown* in 1940.

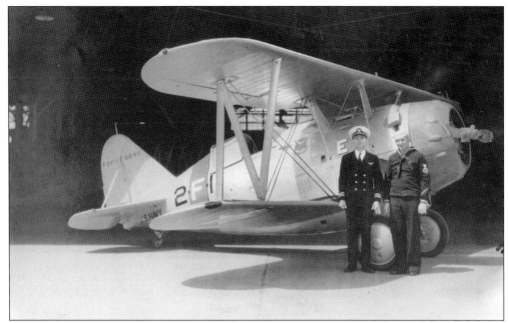

After pioneering naval fighters with retractable landing gear and enclosed cockpits with their FF series, Grumman broke new ground with the F2F-1. This time, the plane was a single-seat biplane and had much better performance. This airplane is from VF-2, known as the "Fighting Chiefs." The squadron was unique in that it was composed almost entirely of enlisted pilots.

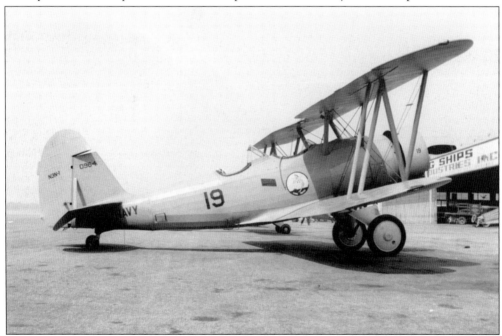

While not based at NAS San Diego, this N3N-1 would have been a regular visitor to the base. Built by the Naval Aircraft Factory in Philadelphia, many were assigned to naval reserve air bases (NRAB). This particular machine was assigned to NRAB Long Beach, a unit that included several movie stars, among them Wallace Beery.

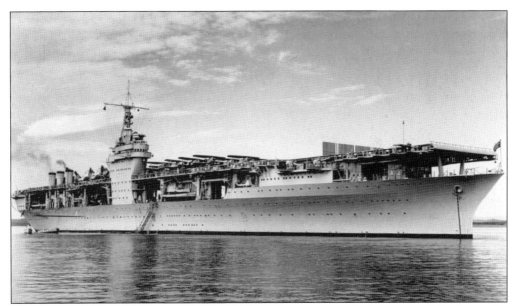

The USS *Ranger* was the fourth aircraft carrier to see service with the navy and the first to be built as a carrier from the keel up. Launched in 1934, and home ported in San Diego until 1939, she was transferred to the Atlantic Fleet and served on neutrality patrol until the outbreak of war. She then provided convoy escort until 1944, when she was reassigned to training duties.

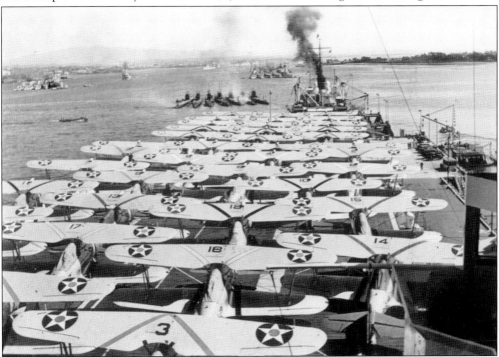

The deck of the USS *Ranger* is packed with aircraft as she sits dockside in San Diego in 1936. The crowded conditions of the flight deck, combined with the roll of the ship at sea, the whirling propellers of the aircraft, and the wind across the deck combined to make it one of the most dangerous places in the world to work. Today's aircraft carrier crew is faced with similar hazards.

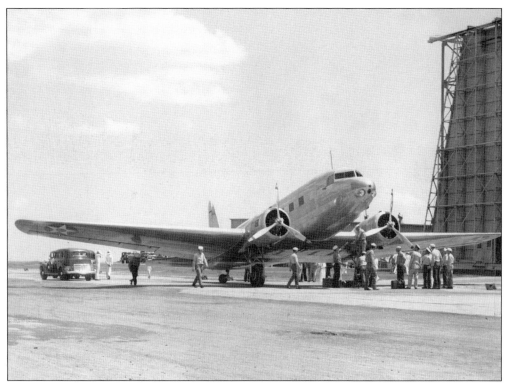

This new Douglas R2D-1 looks sleek and modern in front of the old lighter-than-air hangar at NAS San Diego. Purchased new in 1934, these advanced aircraft replaced the old Ford trimotors and Curtiss Condors.

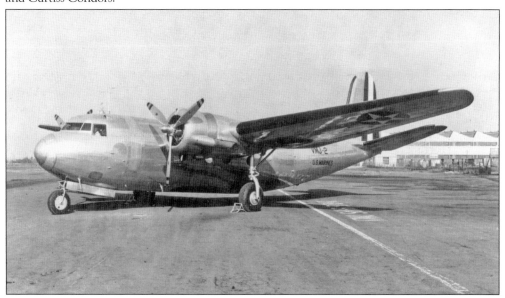

Another modern Douglas transport purchased by the navy was the R3D. Intended as a paratroop transport, the type did not see widespread production but was one of the first tricycle-landing-gear types to be acquired by the navy. This aircraft was photographed at the factory shortly before delivery to VMJ-2 at NAS San Diego.

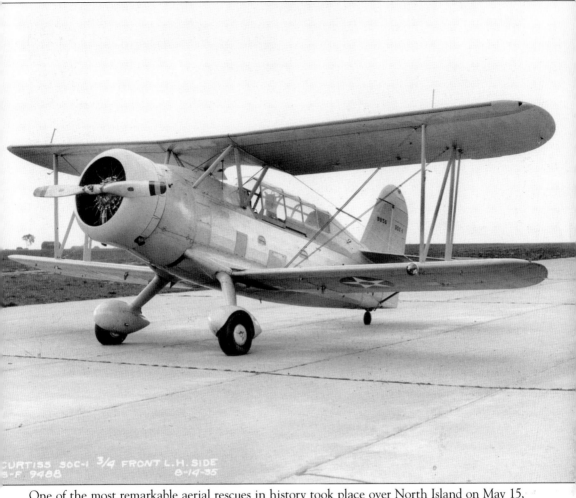

CURTISS SOC-1 ³/₄ FRONT L.H. SIDE
S-F 9488   8-14-35

One of the most remarkable aerial rescues in history took place over North Island on May 15, 1941. Marine paratroopers were doing some training over Camp Kearny north of San Diego. Second Lt. Walter Osipoff became fouled in the static lines trailing behind the plane and ended up being dragged feet first and unconscious underneath the aircraft. Unable to pull him back aboard and with no radio contact with the ground, the transport flew to North Island and circled the tower. Two duty pilots witnessed the scene and leaped into action. Lt. William W. Lowery and Aviation Chief Machinist's Mate John R. McCants jumped into a Curtiss SOC-1 scout plane, like that in the photograph above, and took off. With Lowery at the controls, McCants attempted to pull Osipoff into the rear cockpit. Eventually McCants was able to grasp Osipoff's clothing and pulled him headfirst down between his legs; almost simultaneously, a gust of wind bound the little biplane up, and its propeller blades cut the remaining shrouds holding him. McCants and Lowery were both awarded the Distinguished Flying Cross.

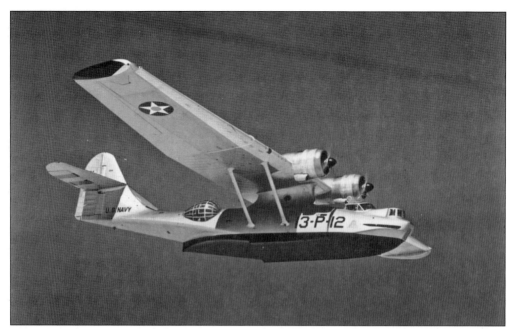

This graceful aircraft is a PBY-4. This particular plane was fitted with PBY-5-style tail surfaces and waist blisters as part of a test program. These features would be present on most of the Catalina aircraft built from that point on. VP-13 operated several different types of aircraft and provided the fleet with tactical training resources from 1939 though the start of the Second World War.

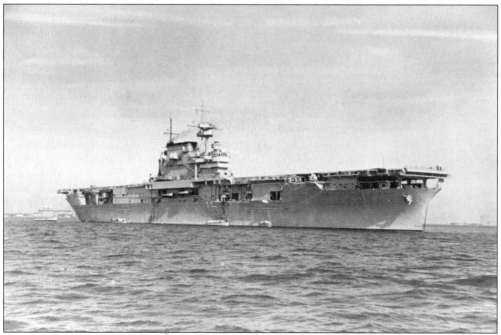

The USS Yorktown, seen here at anchor in San Pedro, was the lead ship of a new class that combined many of the lessons learned from the ships Lexington, Saratoga, and Ranger. Operating on the West Coast from 1939 until the outbreak of war, she gave heroic service until sunk in June 1942 at the conclusion of the Battle of Midway.

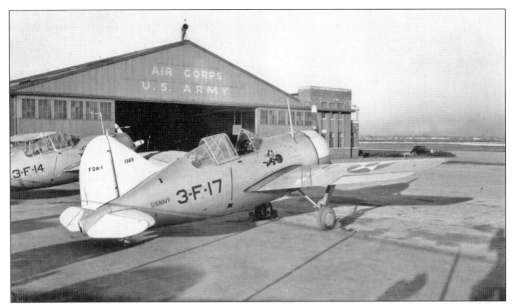

Representing a new generation of naval fighter planes, the all-metal Brewster F2A boasted an enclosed cockpit and retractable landing gear. Capable of speeds well over 300 miles per hour, new monoplanes finally replaced the biplane fighters. This plane is from Fighting Squadron 3 and is seen during a fuel stop on a cross-country flight from San Diego in 1939. VF-3 was assigned to the USS *Saratoga* at the time.

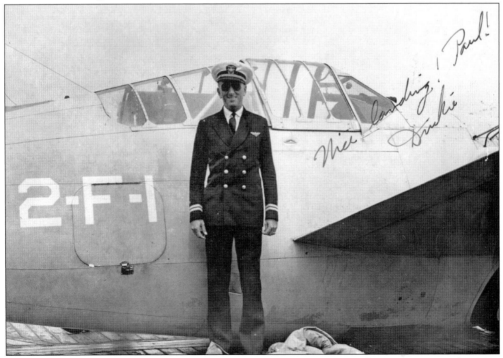

Teething problems, especially with the landing gear, plagued some of the newer types. This VF-2 F2A-3 has suffered a gear failure while operating on board the USS *Lexington* off the San Diego coast in 1941. Some friend of the pilot has written "Nice landing Paul!" on the photograph.

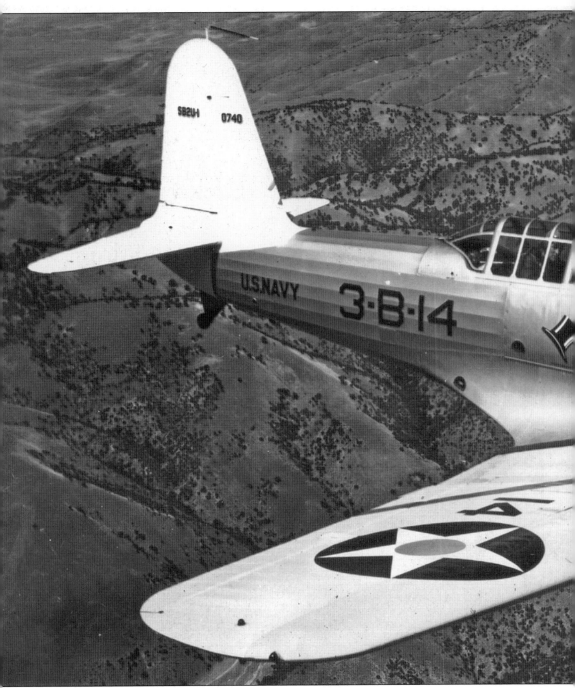

Introduced as a replacement for the biplane dive bomber and scout planes then in service, the Vought SB2U combined a monoplane layout with retractable landing gear. The aircraft was in service from 1936 to 1942. This aircraft is from VB-3. The most colorful era in U.S. naval aviation

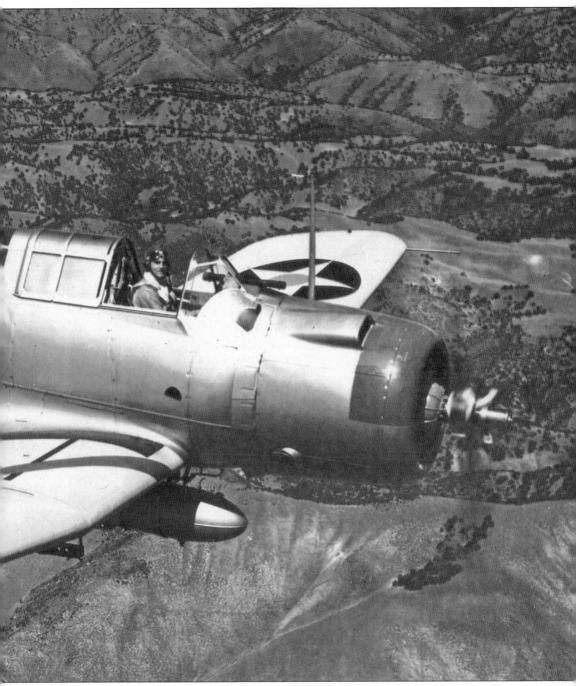

history would soon come to a close. Within a year of this photograph being taken, the chrome yellow wings, silver doped fuselage colored section, and squadron and carrier markings would be painted over with camouflage.

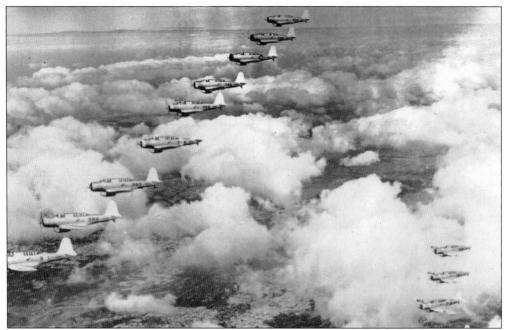

Massed formations of military airplanes were becoming commonplace over San Diego by the late 1930s. Virtually the entire complement of SB2Us from VB-3 off the USS *Saratoga* is seen here with the city spread out below.

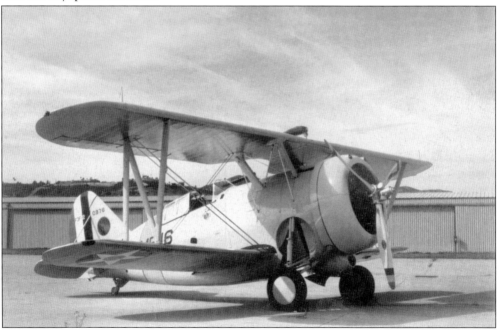

This remarkable airplane is a Grumman F3F-2. It was ditched off the coast of Southern California on August 29, 1940, while providing carrier training for the North Island–based pilots of marine squadron VMF-2. It sat on the ocean bottom until it was accidentally rediscovered in 1988. Recovered in 1991, the plane was fully restored by the craftsmen of the San Diego Air and Space Museum and is now on display at the National Museum of Naval Aviation in Pensacola.

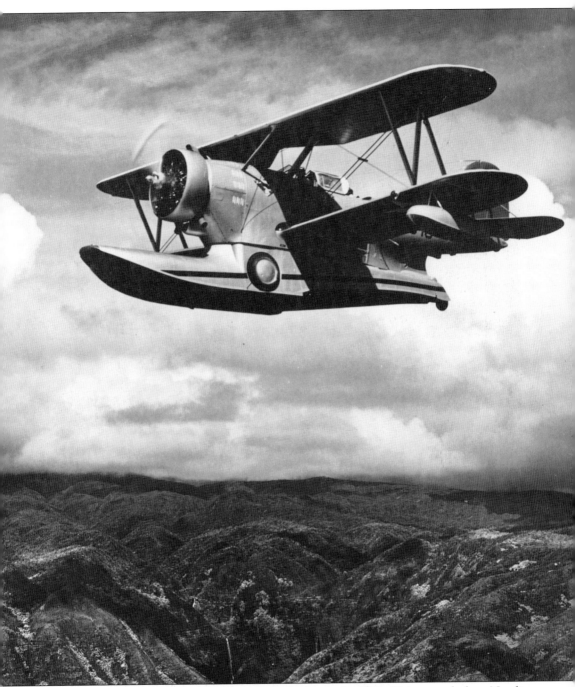

The second production version of the Grumman Duck was the J2F-1. This example from North Island–based VJ-1F is seen flying over San Diego's rugged eastern mountains. The aircraft carried a crew of two but could also accommodate two addition people in the lower fuselage. The biplane Duck represented the end of a glorious era as the U.S. Navy prepared for the global conflict it entered on December 7, 1941.

ACROSS AMERICA, PEOPLE ARE DISCOVERING SOMETHING WONDERFUL. *THEIR HERITAGE.*

Arcadia Publishing is the leading local history publisher in the United States. With more than 3,000 titles in print and hundreds of new titles released every year, Arcadia has extensive specialized experience chronicling the history of communities and celebrating America's hidden stories, bringing to life the people, places, and events from the past. To discover the history of other communities across the nation, please visit:

www.arcadiapublishing.com

Customized search tools allow you to find regional history books about the town where you grew up, the cities where your friends and family live, the town where your parents met, or even that retirement spot you've been dreaming about.

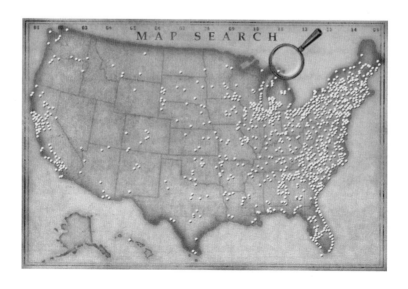